Reality TV

by Shannon Kelly

LUCENT BOOKS
A part of Gale, Cengage Learning

GALE
CENGAGE Learning·

Detroit • New York • San Francisco • New Haven, Conn • Waterville, Maine • London

LIBRARY OF CONGRESS CATALOGING-IN-PUBLICATION DATA

Kelly, Shannon, 1970-
  Reality tv / by Shannon Kelly.
      pages cm. -- (Hot topics)
  Includes bibliographical references and index.
  ISBN 978-1-4205-0905-2 (hardcover)
  1. Reality television programs--History and criticism--Juvenile literature.
I. Title.
  PN1992.8.R43K43 2013
  791.45'6--dc23
                                                                          2012046019

Lucent Books
27500 Drake Rd.
Farmington Hills, MI 48331

ISBN-13: 978-1-4205-0905-2
ISBN-10: 1-4205-0905-5

Printed in the United States of America
2 3 4 5 6 7 17 16 15 14 13

CONTENTS

FOREWORD

Young people today are bombarded with information. Aside from traditional sources such as newspapers, television, and the radio, they are inundated with a nearly continuous stream of data from electronic media. They send and receive e-mails and instant messages, read and write online "blogs," participate in chat rooms and forums, and surf the web for hours. This trend is likely to continue. As Patricia Senn Breivik, the former dean of university libraries at Wayne State University in Detroit, has stated, "Information overload will only increase in the future. By 2020, for example, the available body of information is expected to double every 73 days! How will these students find the information they need in this coming tidal wave of information?"

Ironically, this overabundance of information can actually impede efforts to understand complex issues. Whether the topic is abortion, the death penalty, gay rights, or obesity, the deluge of fact and opinion that floods the print and electronic media is overwhelming. The news media report the results of polls and studies that contradict one another. Cable news shows, talk radio programs, and newspaper editorials promote narrow viewpoints and omit facts that challenge their own political biases. The World Wide Web is an electronic minefield where legitimate scholars compete with the postings of ordinary citizens who may or may not be well-informed or capable of reasoned argument. At times, strongly worded testimonials and opinion pieces both in print and electronic media are presented as factual accounts.

Conflicting quotes and statistics can confuse even the most diligent researchers. A good example of this is the question of whether or not the death penalty deters crime. For instance, one study found that murders decreased by nearly one-third when the death penalty was reinstated in New York in 1995. Death penalty supporters cite this finding to support their argument that the existence of the death penalty deters criminals from committing murder. However, another study found that states without the death penalty have murder rates below the national average. This study is cited by opponents of capital punishment, who reject the claim that the death penalty deters murder. Students need context and clear, informed discussion if they are to think critically and make informed decisions.

The Hot Topics series is designed to help young people wade through the glut of fact, opinion, and rhetoric so that they can think critically about controversial issues. Only by reading and thinking critically will they be able to formulate a viewpoint that is not simply the parroted views of others. Each volume of the series focuses on one of today's most pressing social issues and provides a balanced overview of the topic. Carefully crafted narrative, fully documented primary and secondary source quotes, informative sidebars, and study questions all provide excellent starting points for research and discussion. Full-color photographs and charts enhance all volumes in the series. With its many useful features, the Hot Topics series is a valuable resource for young people struggling to understand the pressing issues of the modern era.

INTRODUCTION

A POWER IN TELEVISION TODAY

When most people think about reality television, what often comes to mind are programs such as *Jersey Shore*, *Keeping Up with the Kardashians*, *American Idol*, and *Survivor*. While these shows certainly qualify as reality television, the genre (category) of reality television includes many other programs that might not be so obvious—everything from game shows such as *The Price Is Right* to documentary-style programs such as *Trauma: Life in the E.R.* and *The First 48* to educational shows such as *Dirty Jobs* and *MythBusters*. Today it seems as if almost every television channel counts at least one or two reality shows on its programming schedule. Even the Weather Channel offers *Coast Guard Alaska* and *Storm Stories*, which air when the station is not covering an immediate, severe weather event. Several channels, such as MTV and Bravo, have very little programming other than reality shows. From 2005 to 2010 an American channel—Fox Reality—was devoted solely to reality programming. Similar channels in Europe and Canada still exist.

A quick glance at the television listings for any day of the week reveals dozens of reality shows that deal with a variety of topics. According to a March 2011 *New York Times* article:

> The genre started as a mix of the moderately silly and the formulaic: survivalist competitions for people willing to eat insects; on-the-job series that followed police officers or ambulance crews. But as the phenomenon expanded

. . . things grew both weirder and more ordinary. On the weird end of the spectrum there were suddenly shows about pathological hoarders and people eaten by their own pets. But there were also shows about people merely doing the everyday: driving a big-rig truck for a living; running a beauty salon.[1]

This expansion reflects a growth in popularity since the genre's modern-day pioneer, MTV's *The Real World*, first aired in 1992. Indeed, according to *Entertainment Weekly*, in the 2010–2011 season, the top ten most-watched programs by those aged eighteen to forty-nine included five reality shows: *American Idol* (both performance and results shows), *The Voice*, *Dancing with the Stars*, and *Survivor: Nicaragua*. (This tally included the first seven days of digital video recorder, or DVR, viewing after an episode aired.) In addition, this list counted only those programs that aired on the five major networks, NBC, CBS, Fox, ABC, and the CW—but reality programs account for a high number of the most-watched shows on cable networks as well. A glance at the top-rated cable programs for the week ending March 4, 2012, finds five reality shows in the top ten: *Jersey Shore*, *Pawn Stars* (which aired twice on that Monday), *Swamp People*, and *Storage Wars*.

These statistics confirm that reality programming is popular. However, the genre is one that is scorned by many who regard it as less worthy than scripted programming. As journalist and TV critic James Poniewozik of *Time* magazine wrote, "It is the one mass-entertainment category that thrives because of its audience's contempt for it. It makes us feel tawdry, dirty, cheap— if it didn't, we probably wouldn't bother tuning in."[2] Part of the problem may be the narrow view mentioned earlier that some people have of what counts as reality programming: It might be easy to think of *The Real Housewives of Atlanta* as a show with little positive value or to be turned off by the endless scheming and double-crossing on *Survivor*, but some consider even these shows worthwhile. Other popular reality programs have more obvious positive traits: *Project Runway* rewards the creativity of its contestants; *Little People, Big World* offers a look into the

Reality TV has grown from a mix of moderately silly and formulaic competitions to big rating makers like American Idol *(shown).*

often-difficult lives of the physically challenged, and *Alaska State Troopers* draws attention to the unique challenges faced by law enforcement in a harsh environment.

The appeal of reality programming, as well as its cultural influence, has been the topic of much debate in recent years. In its early days the genre received little attention from the media. Over time it became clear that reality TV was here to stay and was becoming more wide-reaching in its appeal. Media scholars began to pay attention to reality programming, and it became a major area of academic study. Pop culture is even more reality crazy. A Google search of "reality television" returns a staggering number of pages devoted to the programming and its stars. A search on Kim Kardashian alone nets over 200 million results. Articles about reality television are found in a wide cross section of newspapers and magazines, from the lowbrow to the highbrow, and in early 2012 American Media launched *Reality Weekly*, a new magazine that focuses only on reality programming. Books have been written about reality stars; even serious television news broadcasts offer updates on their networks' reality programming. Reality television seems to have captured the fascination of America, as well as that of other countries around the world.

The question then becomes whether reality television can hold on to that fascination; it has already far outlasted the life expectancy predicted by many media scholars. It remains to be seen if reality programs will continue to snag top slots on the most-watched list. Since 2010, ratings have decreased for some of reality's most well-known hits, such as *American Idol* and *Dancing with the Stars*, causing some to speculate that the end may finally be near. Most people in the entertainment business disagree, however. "Reality TV . . . is here to stay, in that it is simply now another genre of TV, like sitcoms or dramas," says Poniewozik. "But like those other genres, it will have boom times and lean times."[3] And while *Idol*'s ratings have dropped, it was still the highest-rated regularly scheduled entertainment program for seven straight years, until it was replaced as number one during the week of February 9, 2012. And what took its place? Another reality competition show—*The Voice*. With newer shows such as this drawing huge ratings, and old familiars such as *Survivor* and *The Amazing Race* still cracking the top ten on a weekly basis, it seems as if fascination with reality television is still very much a part of today's entertainment culture.

WHAT IS REALITY TELEVISION?

Defining reality television has proved tricky. Indeed, media and communications scholar Kevin Glynn described reality television as "a genre (or more accurately a collection of genres) that is not susceptible to easy definition . . . because of both its internal diversity and its many overlaps with other sets of television genres."[4] Robin Nabi, a Department of Communications professor at the University of California–Santa Barbara and a noted media scholar, wrote a 2003 article with colleagues Erica Biely, Sara Morgan, and Carmen Stitt in which they defined reality television as programs that "film real people as they live out events (contrived or otherwise) in their lives, as these events occur."[5] They further narrowed this definition by saying a program in question must meet certain standards. It must involve people being themselves rather than actors playing characters, the participants must be filmed at least in part in their living or working environment rather than on a production set, the program must not be scripted, the events shown on the program must be placed in a narrative context, and the show must be produced for the main purpose of viewer entertainment.

Nabi and her colleagues' definition seems reasonably clear when applied to shows such as *Big Brother*, in which a group of strangers are placed in a house together and monitored constantly by camera, or to programs that involve live performances, such as *American Idol*. It requires a little more thought, however, to apply that definition to shows such as Syfy's *Destination Truth*, in which a team of adventurers travels the globe in search of mythological creatures and urban legends. According to Nabi, a show being "unscripted" rather than "real" is more likely the most important identifying feature of the genre. This helps to clear up some of the uncertainty when dealing with programs such as *Destination Truth* (although, just to make things more confusing, some of *Destination Truth* and similar shows *is*, in fact, scripted).

Types of Reality Programs

Much like different sources give different definitions for reality television, media scholars do not agree on the various subgroups to include within the genre. One source may list fourteen subgroups; another only ten. One may consider sporting events and talk shows to be reality programming; another may not. Writer and former television producer Michael Essany, in his 2008 book *Reality Check: The Business and Art of Producing Reality TV*, lists twelve subgroups: documentary reality, celebrity reality, competition reality, personal improvement and makeover reality, renovation and design reality, professional reality, forced environment reality, romance reality, aspiration reality, fear-based reality, sports reality, and undercover reality.

Documentary-style reality programs are those that take a "fly-on-the-wall" approach, following events objectively as they occur, with—in theory—little involvement by the production team. *An American Family* in 1973 was an example of this style, as well as current shows *Toddlers and Tiaras*, *Dance Moms*, *Sister Wives*, and *19 Kids and Counting*.

Celebrity reality shows focus on a well-known personality (though rarely an actual A-list star). While many of these shows feature celebrities filmed living their day-to-day lives in a fairly ordinary manner, such as on *Gene Simmons: Family Jewels* or *The Anna Nicole Show*, others situate celebrities in fake environments, such as on *The Surreal Life*, in which a group of celebrities lives together in a mansion while their interactions are filmed and broadcast.

Competition reality shows include both talent-search programs such as *American Idol* and *So You Think You Can Dance* and reality game shows such as *Survivor* and *Fear Factor*. In some cases the audience can affect the outcome of the competition by

In the reality show Big Brother, *a group of strangers lives together while being monitored constantly by video cameras.*

voting for a particular contestant on the show. In others, such as *The Amazing Race*, it is the contestants' own hard work and dedication (or lack thereof) that determine how long they remain in the game.

Personal improvement and makeover reality shows are those in which a person's appearance is supposedly changed for the better. These changes can be slight, such as simply gaining a new wardrobe or hairstyle through *What Not to Wear* or *Queer Eye for the Straight Guy*. Other times they involve changing a person's body, as in the weight-loss competition *The Biggest Loser* or the former Fox show *The Swan*, which offered plastic surgery to those who considered themselves unattractive. The goals of renovation and design reality programs are similar, but for living spaces rather than people. Examples include *Extreme Makeover: Home Edition* and *Trading Spaces.*

Essany divides professional reality programs into two categories: those that focus on people performing their jobs, such as *The First 48* or *Ice Road Truckers*, and those that follow people attempting to achieve success in a certain career, such as *The Apprentice* or *America's Next Top Model.* Forced environment reality shows are those that take strangers and confine them together in a fake environment that is subject to producer manipulation (to manipulate means to alter or influence). *Big Brother* and *The Real World* fall into this category.

DOES REALITY TV HAVE VALUE?

"The sad part of reality television is its exploitive nature. Few, if any, participants are famous because of hard work, talent or skill. They achieve reality stardom because they are willing to expose and exploit a portion of their private lives."—Kelly Boggs, online columnist.

Kelly Boggs. "Reality TV: Why Do People Watch?" Baptist Press, April 8, 2011. www.bp news.net/BPFirstPerson.asp?ID=35022.

Romance reality shows such as *The Bachelor*, *The Bachelorette*, and *Millionaire Matchmaker* attempt to make love connections for or between cast members. Aspiration programs are similar to competition or professional programs except they focus more on the journey toward success and often do not crown an actual winner. Essany provides the example of *Project Greenlight.*

Fear-based reality shows include *Fear* and *Celebrity Paranormal Project*, which both featured participants placed in supposedly haunted environments for a set length of time. Arguably, shows such as *Ghost Hunters*, *Ghost Adventures*, and *Most Haunted* also fall into this category. Sports reality shows are those that feature competitions between athletes. Examples include *The Contender* (boxing), *Ultimate Fighter* (mixed martial arts) and *The Big Break* (golfing). Undercover reality shows are those such as *Off Their Rockers* and *Punk'd*, which film unsuspecting people in unusual situations.

Essany admits there are shows that do not fit easily into any of the subgroups he names. And clearly there is some overlap within subgroups. For example, *Big Brother* is labeled as a forced environment reality show, but it is also a competition since viewers vote people off the show. *Dancing with the Stars* is a reality competition show that features celebrities. *The Biggest Loser* is both a personal makeover show and a competition. *Celebrity Apprentice* might conceivably fit into three categories: professional reality, celebrity reality, and reality competition. This cross-typing is a major reason that scholars find it difficult to agree on an "official" list of reality television subgroups.

The Origins of Reality TV in the United States

The earliest reality television shows were relatively easy to place into categories. Although many people associate reality programming with the 2000s, MTV's *The Real World* in the 1990s is often considered the first example of the genre. But the genre was born even earlier than that. The first game shows to be televised in the United States, *Uncle Jim's Question Bee* and *Truth or Consequences*, debuted in July 1941. Apart from game shows, the first show generally considered to be a reality program was NBC's *Candid Camera*, in which pranks were pulled on unsuspecting participants while hidden cameras recorded their reactions. It first hit the television airwaves in 1948.

The next major milestone in reality television arrived in 1973 with the premiere of *An American Family* on PBS. The twelve-episode series documented seven months in the life of the Louds. The Louds was an upper-middle-class family consisting of parents Bill and Pat Loud and their five children, Lance, Delilah, Grant, Kevin, and Michele. People who tuned in to the show were surprised to find themselves watching the breakup of a marriage, as Pat and Bill's relationship deteriorated before the cameras. The stated goal of following the Louds' lives was to show how an "average" family responded to the daily concerns facing all families at the time. However, many believe producer Craig Gilbert's motive was to draw

Candid Camera

Candid Camera is considered by many media scholars to be the first reality television show. It began as a radio program in 1947 and then moved to ABC's television network in 1948. *Candid Camera* was created by Allen Funt, a New Yorker who attended the Pratt Institute and Cornell and Columbia Universities before landing a job in an advertising agency. The basic idea of the show was to put unsuspecting people in awkward or unusual situations and secretly record their reactions. In one example of a classic stunt, the show rigged a speaker inside a public mailbox, and when a man tried to mail a letter, the box began "talking" to him. When the man attempted to tell a passing policeman about the talking mailbox, it refused to speak. When the prank had run its course, the victim was clued in to what was happening by the show's famous tag line: "Smile! You're on *Candid Camera!*"

Candid Camera ran for nearly sixty years. Allen Funt himself hosted the earlier seasons of the show, with his son Peter joining him and eventually taking over as host in the later seasons.

Allen Funt introduced what many scholars consider the first reality TV show in history with the show Candid Camera.

attention to the greater collapse of traditional American order by showing the downfall of a "typical" American family. When the series began airing, the Louds were strongly criticized by the public and the press, and many of the unkind words were directed at oldest son Lance, who was openly gay.

Real People debuted in 1979 and *That's Incredible!* in 1980. *Real People* featured interviews with people who had unique jobs or hobbies, and *That's Incredible!* highlighted people performing unusual and often dangerous stunts. In the late 1980s reality television began to tackle more serious topics, such as crime and medical emergencies, in programs such as *Unsolved Mysteries* (1987), *America's Most Wanted* (1988), and *Rescue 911* (1989). The year 1989 also saw the debut of *Cops* on Fox. The show, which began its twenty-third season in 2012, follows real-life police officers as they go on patrols and arrest suspects.

The Real World: New York, generally considered to be the modern-day pioneer of reality television, debuted on MTV in 1992. The show features a group of young strangers of different genders, races, religions, backgrounds, and sexual orientations who are selected by the producers to live together in a house (the city varies each season) while their interpersonal relationships are recorded and broadcast. Generally the housemates are also sent on vacations together or given a group project to complete, such as starting a business, in order to highlight their interactions and increase public interest.

While it took some time to familiarize MTV's target audience with the show, it caught on and began drawing 1 million viewers per episode, ushering in a new era in reality television. As Matthew Gilbert of the *Boston Globe* puts it, "*The Real World* was the first time TV told viewers in earnest that ordinary lives could be transformed into lively entertainment programming. Real people had been on game shows, talent contests, and documentaries, but the . . . idea that they could star as dramatic or comic figures with their own plot arcs was new."[6]

Early seasons of *The Real World* were praised by the media for their willingness to openly explore topics such as prejudice, sexuality, abortion, addiction, and political and religious differences. Later seasons, however, have been criticized as simply a showcase for bad behavior, drinking, fighting, and casual sex. Reality TV critic Andy Denhart believes that bad behavior has always been a part of the show but that the motivations for that behavior have changed: "What once was the result of relationships between people with different backgrounds has become behavior from people who know they will get more attention and become more famous the more outrageously they act."[7] While many of the original fans have deserted the show because of this shift in tone, it still draws enough viewers to satisfy MTV. The show's twenty-seventh season, *The Real World: St. Thomas* aired in 2012.

REALITY TV EXCITES AND ENTERTAINS

"Reality TV—call it 'discomfort TV'—lives to rattle viewers' cages. It provokes. It offends. But at least it's trying to do something besides help you get to sleep."—James Poniewozik, journalist and TV critic.

James Poniewozik. "Why Reality TV Is Good for Us." *Time*, February 12, 2003. www .time.com/time/magazine/article/0,9171,421047,00.html.

In 1999 the game show *Who Wants to Be a Millionaire?* was adapted from the British version and hit the American airwaves. Viewers were excited by the show because ordinary people—not just those with genius IQ levels—could qualify as contestants simply by calling a number and answering a few questions. In its first season *Millionaire* was so popular that ABC aired it five times a week. The show had close to 30 million viewers per episode and actually altered phone traffic in the United States. According to Mark Andrejevic in *Reality TV: The Work of Being Watched*, "By early 2000, the telephone company noted that the standard lull in telephone activity in the evening (post-work) hours was interrupted by a jagged peak at 10 P.M. (Eastern time), representing the thousands of phone calls made to the *Who Wants to Be a Millionaire* hotline at the end of the show."[8] The show's ratings began to decline steadily after its second season, however, and its prime-time version was canceled in 2002.

In 2000 CBS premiered *Survivor* and *Big Brother*, and in 2001 it began airing *The Amazing Race*. *Survivor*, which completed its twenty-fourth season in 2012, features a group of strangers placed in the wilderness, divided into tribes, and tasked with providing food, water, and shelter for themselves. They also compete in challenges to earn rewards or to gain immunity from being voted off the show by their fellow contestants. The ultimate winner of the show, the last survivor standing, receives a prize of $1 million. *Big Brother*, which aired its fourteenth season in 2012, is similar to *The Real World* in that it places a group of strangers together in a house and monitors them constantly with cameras. However, on *Big Brother* the Houseguests, as they are called, are completely isolated from the outside world and interact only with one another for the three months it takes to film the show. Each week a combination of votes from the public and the other Houseguests evicts one person from the house, and the contestant who remains at the end wins five hundred thousand dollars. On *The Amazing Race*, teams of two compete in a race around the world, performing various challenges and tasks—everything from skydiving to beard styling—along the way and trying to finish ahead of the other teams. Typically, the last team to finish a leg (episode) of the race is eliminated (cut) from the competition, and the winning team takes home $1 million. The show finished its twenty-first season in December 2012.

After the appearance of these three series, reality programming blossomed. *Trading Spaces* hit the air in 2000 and produced a subgenre of home-makeover shows. *The Bachelor*, which features an attractive single man attempting to choose a mate from among a pool of female contestants, appeared in 2002. Celebrity-based shows took off that same year with the premiere of *The Osbournes*. *American Idol* also debuted in 2002, leading a wave of competition shows that included *America's Next Top Model* (2003), *The Apprentice* (2004), *Dancing with the Stars* (2005), and *So You Think You Can Dance* (2006).

Survivor features a group of strangers divided into "tribes," placed in a wilderness setting, and tasked with providing food, water, and shelter for themselves while competing with each other to be the last person left after everyone else is voted out.

Reality Programming in Europe

The era of reality programming had begun in earnest, and it was certainly not limited to the United States. In fact, many of the most well-known American reality shows are versions of programs that began in foreign countries—many from Europe. For example, *Expedition Robinson*, which debuted in Sweden in 1997 and is currently back on the air, provided the model for *Survivor*. *Big Brother* actually originated in the Netherlands in 1999. *The Voice* is an adaptation of *The Voice of Holland*. *Dancing with the Stars* is based on the British program *Strictly Come Dancing*. Britain's *Pop Idol*, which first aired in 2001, gave birth to *American Idol* as well as similar versions in numerous other countries. Indeed, Britain is responsible for a large number of reality television exports, supplying 43 percent of global entertainment formats in early 2011.

Lately, however, according to the *Economist*, the British public has begun to turn away from the typical reality shows that

Early Lessons from *The Real World*

Pedro Zamora was a participant on MTV's *The Real World: San Francisco*, the third installment in the *Real World* series that aired in 1994. Zamora, a Cuban American, was one of the first openly gay men to appear in a television series. He was also an AIDS educator who was himself living with the disease. Probably the best-known person to appear on the show, Zamora opened the eyes of many MTV viewers to the risks of AIDS as he taught his fellow house members about the illness. These viewers also saw a loving, dedicated gay relationship between Zamora and his boyfriend, Sean Sasser, which was highlighted with an emotional commitment ceremony performed before the show's cameras.

Zamora died at the age of twenty-two on November 11, 1994—the day after the last episode of *The Real World: San Francisco* aired. President Bill Clinton praised Zamora for his work as an AIDS activist and called the young man to offer support when Zamora was hospitalized after the show finished filming. Clinton introduced the premiere of *Pedro*, a 2009 biopic of Zamora, with the words: "To this day, Pedro Zamora remains an extraordinary example of what a huge impact one young person can make in our world."

Quoted in Hal Boedecker. "Reality Star's Riveting Message Still Resonates in Film." *Orlando Sentinel*, April 1, 2009. http://articles.orlandosentinel.com/2009-04-01/news/pedro01_1_pedro-zamora-alex-loynaz-real-world.

place cast members in fake environments and to show more interest in reality-based programs. Two examples are *24 Hours in A&E*, a documentary-style show about the happenings at King's College Hospital, and *One Born Every Minute*, which focuses on couples dealing with childbirth. Programs that mix real behavior with some scripted moments (called "soft-scripted" shows) have also begun to gain favor. Two such programs are *Made in Chelsea*, which focuses on the young social elite of London's Chelsea district, and *The Only Way Is Essex*, which follows a group of party promoters, models, and club managers in well-to-do Essex County outside London. Despite these new interests, however, many of the most-watched reality shows in the United Kingdom are still titles that are familiar to Americans, such as *The Voice UK* and *Britain's Got Talent*.

Most European countries have versions of the most well-known reality shows, such as *Survivor*, *Big Brother*, *MasterChef*, and *Idol*. But there are programs unique to each country as well. France, for example, has *Rendez-vous en Terre Inconnue* (*See You in a Strange Land*), in which a group of participants is taken to a secret location and given two weeks to adapt to the native lifestyle. Germany has *Daniela Katzenberger: Natürlich Blond* (*Naturally Blond*), which features Daniela Katzenberger, a singer and model. Katzenberger's on-camera personality, which has been labeled as "ditzy," has led some to call her the "German Paris Hilton."

Reality TV in Asia

Although reality programming may be readily available in Europe, it is far less common in Asian countries. In some cases it is a target of government censorship. Recently, one Chinese reality dating show, *Fei Cheng Wu Rao* (*If You Were the One*), created so much controversy that state officials changed the country's broadcasting regulations. The show features a panel of women who ask a potential male suitor questions, and officials were concerned that the behavior of the participants did not support traditional Chinese values. Concern rose sharply after one female contestant said she would rather "cry in a BMW" than go on a bicycle ride with the male participant. The State Administration of Radio, Film, and Television (SARFT) issued an edict that declared: "Do not humiliate and assault participants in the name of dating; do not discuss vulgar topics involving sex; do not hype materialism and other unhealthy, incorrect viewpoints on marriage; and do not air the show without censorship and editing."[9]

Changes were made to the show to bring it more in line with what the officials considered appropriate: The young female contestants were all replaced with older, more disciplined ones, talk of how much money the participants made was cut out, and each episode was reviewed six times by censors before it could air. SARFT was still not satisfied, however, and passed a law that only two entertainment shows (defined in China as dating shows, game shows, or celebrity talk shows) could be broadcast per television station per week, with the total number allowed per night at nine, or sixty-three per week. Before this, the number of entertainment shows aired per week was thought to be 126, so the new law resulted in a major decrease in reality programming.

Another Chinese reality show, a popular talent competition called *Super Girl*, was canceled in 2011 after an eight-year run. The official reason offered for the cancellation was that the program was running over its allotted screen time. Popular belief, however, held that the censors targeted the show because they thought it had a morally corrupting influence. Li Hao, the spokesperson for the channel that aired *Super Girl*, stated, "Instead, the channel will air programs that promote moral ethics and public safety and provide practical information for housework."[10]

One of the shows China considers more appropriate for its citizens is *Who Is the Ultimate Hero?*, which features members of the People's Liberation Army who are pitted against each other in tasks such as target shooting and descending from cliffs and buildings using ropes. Another is *Legal Editorial Department*, which focuses on episodes of fraud, adultery, and murder and the punishments a person might face for committing these crimes.

As for reality television in other Asian countries, Japan is well known for its wacky game shows, some of which have been adapted for other countries. It also features shows such as Fuji TV's *Ainori 2* (*Ride Together 2*), in which singles travel around the world in a pink bus and try to make romantic connections with each other while learning about other countries. MTV Asia also recently began airing *Shibuhara Girls*, which features young Japanese women seeking success in the pop culture and fashion industries. *Infinite Challenge* is a Korean show in which contestants compete in weekly challenges, most of which are silly or impossible to achieve.

Indonesia has produced a fair number of reality programs, although that number has begun to decrease in recent years. Popular shows in that country include *Jika Aku Menjadi* (*If I Were*), which sends wealthy citizens to aid poor Indonesians in rural areas, and *Minta Tolong* (*Ask for Help*), a hidden-camera show that films unsuspecting people to determine whether or not they are worthy of receiving a reward. In India and Pakistan creators hope that reality shows might heal some of the

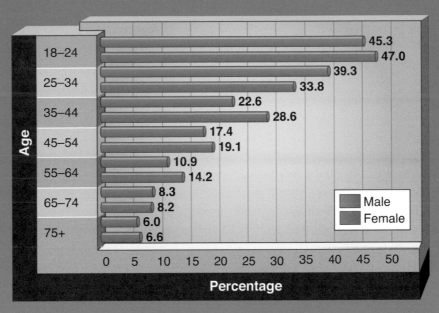

Percentage Who Watch Reality Television Frequently, by Age/Sex

Age		
18–24	45.3	47.0
25–34	39.3	33.8
35–44	22.6	28.6
45–54	17.4	19.1
55–64	10.9	14.2
65–74	8.3	8.2
75+	6.0	6.6

Male
Female

Percentage

Taken from: MARS Survey. www.zonacatino.com/zldata302.htm.

bad blood between the two rival countries. *Foodistan* pits Indian and Pakistani chefs against each other, while *Musical Battlefield* does the same with musicians. Success so far, however, has been limited, since the top Pakistani chef on *Foodistan* quit the show before the season's end after claiming the judges favored the Indian contestants.

Reality TV in the Arab World

Perhaps surprisingly, reality television even exists in historically conservative Arab countries governed by strict customs about what is appropriate and what is not. Most of these programs seek to appeal to the younger members of the population, who are not afraid to push limits and embrace more progressive values. As Joe Kalil, a communications professor in Qatar, explains, "The shows are trying to say to this young and vibrant group who wants to learn, wants to be entertained: 'This is you. This is your culture. These are your values and your decisions. Make them count.'"[11]

One of the most popular reality shows in the Arab world is *Star Academy*, which debuted in 2003. Contestants are selected from a variety of Arab countries to live together in a penthouse (from which footage is aired on a satellite channel around the clock) and perform weekly for viewer votes. Talent is not limited to singing; some contestants dance or act. The Arab world also had its own version of *American Idol*, which was called *Super Star*. Other programs have included a home-makeover show, *Labor and Materials*, in which houses destroyed during the war in Iraq were rebuilt, and even an Arab version of *The Bachelorette* called *Ala al-Hawa Sawa*.

These shows have had their share of controversy. In the first season of *Super Star*, the competition spilled over from the contestants to their countries of origin, turning it into what one newspaper article called a "battle of nations." The three semi-finalists were a Lebanese man, a Syrian man, and a Jordanian

China's popular show Super Girl *was canceled by the Chinese government, which purportedly thought it had a morally corrupting influence.*

woman. When the Lebanese man was cut, fans in both the studio and Lebanon's capital city of Beirut rioted because many believed that the elimination was the result of Syrian political pressure. Then, during the week prior to the finale, Jordan's King Abdullah asked his country's citizens to text votes for the Jordanian contestant and said the government would pay for the texting. The Jordanian, Diana Karazon, won.

The Lebanon-based *Star Academy* created even more problems. According to author Naomi Sakr, "[The show's] popularity prompted Lebanese restaurant owners to complain about decreased dinner business, Saudi clerics to issue religious rulings [ordering] Muslims to boycott it, Kuwaiti politicians to launch parliamentary inquiries into media policies that allowed *Star Academy* broadcasts, and fans and [critics] to set up websites about the programme."[12] The show was seen by religious conservatives as a bad influence on the population. A particular source of criticism stemmed from the fact that unmarried men and women lived together in the penthouse and that footage from all rooms of the house (including bedrooms) was aired. Mixed-gender communal living is considered inappropriate in many Middle Eastern countries. Another show, an Arab version of *Big Brother* called *Al-Ra'is*, handled the same situation by housing its male and female participants separately and having a daily call to prayer. Protests still broke out, however, and it was canceled after only a few episodes.

Reality TV in the Rest of the World

Some reality programs in Africa have also created controversy over what is seen as inappropriate behavior in African culture. The main issue has focused on *Big Brother Africa*, which has been accused of presenting immoral behavior to Africa's youth. African countries offer fewer reality shows than many of their counterparts on other continents, and most of them, like *Big Brother Africa*, are versions of European shows, including *Survivor: Africa* and several versions of *Idol*. Some original programs exist, however, such as *Project: Inspire Africa*, a show that rewards entrepreneurship (business creation and management) in young Africans, and *Ready for Marriage Extraordinary*, in which former prostitutes attempt to find husbands.

Critics claim Big Brother Africa *presents immoral behavior to African youth.*

Australian reality programming features many recognizable European and American titles as well. In 2012 the five nominees for Most Popular Reality Program category of the Logie Awards (the Australian television industry awards) were *MasterChef: Australia*, *My Kitchen Rules*, *Beauty and the Geek Australia*, *X-Factor Australia*, and *The Block* (which features four couples competing to renovate a house and sell it for the highest price at auction). In Canada much of the reality programming consists of rebroadcasts of American shows and Canadian versions of the usual standbys, such as *So You Think You Can Dance Canada* and *Canada's Next Top Model*. Some original programs are found on the country's cable channels, however.

Some Central and South American countries feature original programs as well. For example, Mexico has *Iniciativa Mexico* (*Initiative Mexico*), a program that focuses on improving the welfare of the population. On the show, twenty-five activists compete for $2.5 million to pay for programs they believe will aid the country's poor. Brazil recently debuted *Mulheres Ricas* (*Rich Women*), which focuses on the lives of five of the country's female millionaires. The show created instant debate because the country is considered one of the most economically unequal societies in the world. The *Guardian* reported that while the country has created nineteen millionaires a day since 2007, more than 11 million Brazilians live in slums.

It seems that reality shows have invaded almost every part of the globe. Producers throughout the world are drawn to reality programming because of its recognition factor, its low production costs, and the relatively brief time needed to produce an entire season. These factors have combined to allow billions of viewers the chance to become obsessed with a genre that some believe has, in the words of one journalist, "eaten television whole."[13]

CHAPTER 2

WHY DO PEOPLE WATCH REALITY TELEVISION?

Reality television has undoubtedly become a major lure for television viewers. Reality shows have topped the ratings list of most-watched programs among eighteen- to forty-nine-year-olds for over a decade. Clearly the genre has wide appeal. But why? Who watches reality programs? What, if any, traits do they have in common? Reality shows draw viewers from all major statistical groups—age, sex, class, race, and so forth—and studies indicate that people watch reality shows for a variety of reasons.

The Appeal of Ourselves

One reason offered for the popularity of reality television is that viewers relate to the contestants because the contestants seem like ordinary people, very much like the viewers themselves. Author Eric Jaffe, commenting on the 51 million viewers who tuned in to the *Survivor* finale in 2000, said, "By watching in such high numbers, viewers told network executives to dump their high-priced writers and lovely actors in favor of identifiable people in familiar conflicts. All we really wanted to see was the same thing we saw in the mirror every morning—ourselves. Only different."[14]

People might also enjoy imagining themselves in the place of the cast members on reality shows. A study published in the *Journal of Consumer Research* in 2005 found that viewers often like to imagine what they would do if placed in the same situation or faced with the same problem as a participant in a reality program they watched. This process of social comparison with the reality participant helps viewers define their own values and beliefs.

Although some media scholars theorize that people watch reality television to fantasize about becoming well-known, other scholars disagree. Psychology professor Bryant Paul, for example, believes that the fact that the participants on many reality shows are so ordinary lessens the need for viewers themselves to become famous. According to Bryant, "The fact that these [reality show participants] were not groomed for celebrity in the traditional sense, that friends of friends invariably went to camp with someone on one of the shows, is the great draw. The closer someone is to you, the easier it is to empathize . . . and really good empathy equals really good television."[13]

Surreal Life cast members MC Hammer, left; Gabrielle Carteris, center; and Brande Roderick talk about the show to the press. Celebrity reality shows are popular because people like to watch celebrities just being themselves, which makes them seem more human and approachable.

Reality Television: The Great Equalizer

What, then, is the appeal of reality programs that feature established celebrities rather than people pulled from the ranks of the unknown? Shows such as *The Surreal Life*, *Being Bobby Brown*, and *Kathy Griffin: My Life on the D-List* have drawn viewers curious to peek into the lives of the rich and famous. People find comfort in the fact that famous people are, at the core, very similar to themselves, with the same concerns and problems—which money and/or fame cannot always solve. Watching celebrities perform everyday tasks helps the average person relate to them and helps viewers feel better about their own lives.

One of the most well-known celebrity-based programs was MTV's *The Osbournes*, which documented the lives of controversial heavy metal singer Ozzy Osbourne and his family, considered odd by many. David S. Escoffery, attempting to explain the appeal of the series, wrote:

> In one short scene from the first episode of Season One, Ozzy sees some trash on the kitchen floor and goes to throw it away. He is unhappy to find that all three of the kitchen trash cans have no bags in them. Grumbling, he finds trash bags and re-lines the cans. It is such a simple act, one that normal people do all the time. However, seeing Ozzy Osbourne replacing trash bags, especially with silly whistling music in the background, really brings him down to our level.[16]

Many of the celebrities who appear on reality shows are lower-tier entertainers that the media culture invests less time and interest in, which appears to be the way viewers prefer it. This may be because major stars are simply seen as too "different" for the average viewer to identify with at all. Many star participants were well-known at some point in the past, but then faded from public view until they popped up unexpectedly on a reality show. In some cases such an appearance can revive the star's career. Lead singer Bret Michaels of Poison had mostly disappeared from the public's view until he reappeared in the VH1 show *Rock of Love*. After that appearance, he was asked to perform on *Good Morning*

America and the always celebrity-studded final episode of *American Idol*. Michaels also became the winning contestant on *Celebrity Apprentice 3* in 2010. Ozzy Osbourne's popularity was likewise refreshed once *The Osbournes* began to air.

Another reason that celebrity reality shows draw viewers is because celebrities in general provide a shared cultural experience among members of a population. As Christopher Bell points out in his book *American Idolatry*, shared cultural references are becoming harder to come by as the number of entertainment options people have increases, making it more difficult for people to bond over one particular book, film, or television show. As Bell puts it, "Celebrities provide cultural touchstones at the same time they serve as cultural totems for how (and how not) to behave. We may not all care when Brad Pitt and Angelina Jolie produce (or, more likely, adopt) a new child, but almost all of us know that it happened."[17]

ARE PEOPLE WATCHING FOR THE WRONG REASONS?

"Reality television plays to people's worst instincts and depends on people behaving badly, manipulating others, lying and violence. The mere suggestion that a teenage girl bashing up the father of her child is somehow entertaining; well there is something wrong with that."—Matt Philbin, managing editor of the Culture and Media Institute.

Quoted in Hollie McKay. "Reality Shows Aimed at Young Viewers Airing More Violent Scenes." Fox News, October 11, 2010. www.foxnews.com/entertainment/2010/10/11/reality-shows-battery-domestic-violence-jersey-shore-teen-mom.

One shared cultural experience that results in the popularity of a reality show is nostalgia. Producers take advantage of the willingness of viewers to tune in to a show to find out the latest about someone who may have been well known and well liked in the past. For example, some viewers were eager to see Ralph Macchio, a teen heartthrob in the 1980s, when he competed on *Dancing with the Stars* in 2011. Indeed, *Dancing*, which recruits actors, athletes, singers, and other personalities to pair with ballroom dancing pros and compete against each other, often draws viewers eager to see what a particular celebrity looks like or has been up to since dropping out of the spotlight. In recent years the popularity of some of these shows has resulted in their ability to draw a higher level of celebrity talent than in their early seasons.

America's Got Talent

Another reason people watch talent competitions such as *Dancing with the Stars* is straightforward: They are sometimes rewarded with outstanding performances. For every terrible audition the viewer is forced to endure on *American Idol*, there is someone like Adam Lambert earning a standing ovation from cranky judge Simon Cowell for "Mad World" or an unknown Fantasia Barrino moving the audience to tears with "Summertime." These are the so-called water cooler moments that people talk about the next day at work or school, and viewers are excited to be a part of the discussion. *The Voice* eliminates the bad auditions altogether, showcasing only those with real talent. *So You Think You Can Dance* also produces moments of brilliance, and its routines are often nominated for Emmys in the category of Best Choreography.

In addition to enjoying the performances, viewers also know they can directly affect the lives of the participants with their votes. This allows viewers to feel involved in the program and provides a sense of power. As voiced by communications professor S. Shyam Sundar, speaking during *Idol*'s reign at the top of the ratings chart, "No longer mere couch potatoes in front of their boob tubes, viewers join the creative production; the experience feels less like simply watching television and more like being part of a shared national project. *American Idol* is the most popular television show in America not because it produces stars . . . but because it turns audience members into what they always wanted to be: star-makers."[18] By simply dialing a phone number or sending a text message, a viewer is able to support a needy contestant—say a struggling single parent or a cancer survivor—and help change that person's life for the better.

Of course, not all performances on these shows are worthy of praise, which is just fine with some viewers. Some people

American Idol

American Idol is one of the best-known and most influential reality programs on the air. It has had a very strong effect on both American popular culture and the entertainment industry. Indeed, in 2007 NBC chief executive Jeff Zucker claimed that *Idol* has had the greatest impact of any show in television's history. The other networks call it a ratings monster and fear having to air shows against it. Even though its numbers have decreased some in recent years, millions of people still watch the show and call in to vote. During the show's fifth-season finale, host Ryan Seacrest announced that the number of votes cast for the winner was higher than the number of votes cast for any president in U.S. history.

Many of *Idol*'s contestants have gone on to successful careers in the music industry. Carrie Underwood, for example, has become one of the top-selling country artists in the business, and first-season winner Kelly Clarkson has sold millions of albums and won numerous awards. Jennifer Hudson, who did not even win her season of *Idol*, nonetheless won a Grammy Award and later branched out into acting, winning an Oscar for her performance in the 2006 film *Dreamgirls*.

Former American Idol *contestant Jennifer Hudson went on to win a Grammy and an Oscar for her performance in the 2006 film* Dreamgirls.

tune in specifically to gawk at bad auditions and shake their heads in disgust at singers whom they believe should not be allowed anywhere near a karaoke machine in their own living room, much less a national stage. They get a sense of personal satisfaction from thinking, "I might not be a terrific singer, but I can sing better than *that*," or "I would never humiliate myself in front of millions of people like that person is doing." Viewers also might enjoy watching the judges scold contestants about a bad performance.

Embarrassment as Entertainment?

This attitude highlights another reason why some people watch reality programming of *all* types—to make fun of the people on the shows, feel superior to them, or experience feelings of *schaden-freude*. (*Schadenfreude* means "happiness at the misfortune of others.") As Sandra Gonzalez, a writer for the website Television Without Pity, puts it:

> I understand that all of the popular reality shows have some sort of unexplainable power to capture our attention. We watch *Big Brother* for the (sometimes poorly) veiled sexual innuendos hidden in the competitions and to mock dumb contestants. We watch *The Bachelor* because we're secretly hopeless romantics who like to mock dumb contestants. We watch *Survivor* because, well, it's sometimes a really good game . . . and to mock dumb contestants.[19]

According to clinical psychologist Geoffrey White, viewers enjoy identifying with a cast member who is humiliating another and knowing at the same time that they are not actually responsible for the suffering that results. And in a sense it appears to be harmless behavior on the part of viewers: The viewers do not know the people they are making fun of, nor do they have any direct contact with them, so how are they hurting them? Of course, in this day and age, the average viewer *can* have personal communication, of a sort, with a person on a television show, thanks to social media and the Internet. Some reality show participants have Twitter accounts that viewers can follow and post comments to, which sometimes results in the celebrity responding. Other television personalities may read and address comments that viewers post about them in the forums on entertainment websites.

It may be that this *schadenfreude* is less mean-spirited than it seems at first. White also points out that in uncertain times, when the population is feeling uneasy or unsettled, seeing that others are suffering as well might serve as a source of comfort. Indeed, many people claim to watch reality television because it makes them feel better about their own lives—they may have problems, but at least they are not living in a house filled to the roof with garbage or dealing with an unwanted teen pregnancy.

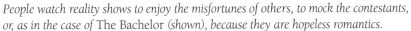

People watch reality shows to enjoy the misfortunes of others, to mock the contestants, or, as in the case The Bachelor *(shown), because they are hopeless romantics.*

Reality programs help put things in perspective for these viewers. And while they may laugh about the bad decisions made by reality show participants, viewers might also learn from them—and hope the participants will learn something as well. As *Jersey Shore* fan Sydney Lipez admits, "I do look for redeeming qualities in these people . . . and I root for them. I want to find out that they're not as stupid as I think."[20]

In addition, research has found that many viewers do not enjoy seeing others embarrassed on television. In one study of the show *Survivor*, the researcher found that of the study participants, "none found appeal in watching cast members being [shunned] or voted off the show. In fact, reactions were exactly the opposite, as voiced by this group member: 'Some of the times that seem to trouble me the most is when someone's being humiliated. I don't really like that.'"[21]

Some scholars suggest that what may keep some people from watching reality shows is not the fact that people on them are often made to look foolish, but that those people are sometimes unaffected by, or even unaware of, the fact that their actions look bad to viewers. On the twentieth season of *The Amazing Race*, team members Brendon and Rachel whine and complain their way through Italy's Turin, their arguments spiraling to the point that Rachel dramatically threatens to throw herself into oncoming traffic. Yet as millions of viewers at home roll their eyes, Brendon and Rachel seem completely unaware of how childish their behavior may appear to those watching. A lack of self-consciousness is not *always* a bad thing, however—and everyone can learn from the embarrassment suffered by cast members on reality shows. As journalist and TV critic James Poniewozik points out:

> For all the talk about "humiliation TV," what's striking about most reality shows is how good humored and resilient most of the participants are: the *American Idol* rejectees stubbornly convinced of their own talent, the *Fear Factor* players walking away from vats of insects like Olympic champions. . . . Embarrassment, these shows demonstrate, is survivable, even ignorable, and ignoring embarrassment is a skill we could all use. It is what you risk—like injury in a sport—in order to triumph.[22]

Tom Rogan, executive producer of TLC's *Here Comes Honey Boo Boo*, which chronicles the antics of seven-year-old pageant participant Alana Thompson and her family, agrees. In defending the show's tendency to air unflattering moments that other shows might cut, he stated of the Thompson family, "This is the important part: they're not embarrassed or ashamed about it . . . they're very comfortable with it." He went on to say it was "'refreshing' for his team to find cast members they didn't have to protect."[23]

The First Nabi Study

One of the first important academic studies to focus on reasons why people watch reality television was the 2003 study that was conducted by communications professor Robin Nabi and her colleagues. In the study, Nabi and her colleagues investigated whether there was truth to the theory that people watched reality programs to satisfy voyeuristic tendencies. Voyeurism in this case was mainly defined as deriving personal pleasure from peeking into the lives of other people.

VIEWER CURIOSITY

"Watching real people on TV is fascinating, just like watching people in the airport is fascinating. Viewers are interested in people—not pain."—Robin Nabi, media scholar.

Quoted in Eric Jaffe. "Reality Check." *Observer*, March 2005. www.psychologicalscience.org/observer/getArticle.cfm?id=1742.

The study was conducted on 252 residents of Tucson, Arizona, who appeared for jury duty. The participants completed a survey that measured their personality traits, their overall television viewing patterns, their exposure to several reality television programs, and their thoughts on one particular reality program of which they were either a regular or casual viewer. The results showed that the top three reasons that regular viewers of reality programming watched was because they found the programs entertaining, found the programs suspenseful, and enjoyed the

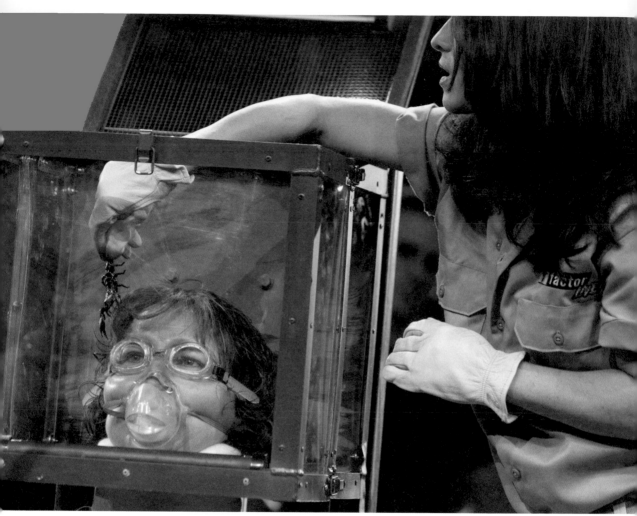

A woman has live scorpions placed on her head on the show Fear Factor. *Some reality shows demonstrate that embarrassment is survivable and that overcoming embarrassment is a skill that everyone can use.*

unscripted nature of reality shows. Casual viewers—those who only tuned in to a reality program once in awhile—reported they liked to watch out of a sense of curiosity and for entertainment. The desire for voyeurism, although present, was not found to be the major reason people watched reality programs. Rather than wanting to peek inside people's personal lives just to be nosy, viewers were more interested in feeling connected to others and gaining personal insight about the human condition. Nabi and her colleagues ended their study with the recommendation that future research focus on what might specifically cause a viewer to find a program entertaining and gain emotional enjoyment from it.

The Reiss Study

This issue was soon addressed by psychologist and professor Steven Reiss and his colleague James Wiltz. In 2000 Reiss had suggested a theory to explain human motivation. This theory states that there are sixteen basic desires that guide human behavior. The sixteen desires are: independence, curiosity, power, honor, idealism, saving (the storing of supplies/possessions), acceptance, order, romance, vengeance (the desire to get even), family, status, social contract (the desire to be with peers), physical activity, eating, and tranquility. Reiss explains that a person strongly motivated by social contract is often looking for chances to socialize, whereas a person with a weak desire for social contract most likely will not even be aware of who is having a party that weekend. According to Reiss, "These desires are what drive our everyday actions and make us who we are. . . . What makes individuals unique is the combination and ranking of these desires."[24]

In 2004, shortly after the results of Nabi's study were published, Reiss and Wiltz applied this theory of sixteen basic desires to viewers of reality television in an effort to explain the appeal of these shows. Their study involved 239 adults who were either employed in human services fields or were students at a Midwestern university. The study participants completed a 159-question booklet. The questions measured their participation in and enjoyment of various forms of travel and entertainment (including reality television) and asked them to rank each of Reiss's sixteen desires in order of importance to them.

The results of the study indicated that status—or the greater-than-usual wish to feel self-important—was the main motivation for reality television viewing. According to a *Psychology Today* article by Reiss and Wiltz, "The desire for status is just a means to get attention. And more attention increases one's sense of self-importance: We think we are important if others pay attention to us and unimportant if ignored."[25] They further explained how watching reality programs might help fulfill that desire:

> One possibility is that viewers feel they are more important (have higher status) than the ordinary people portrayed on reality television shows. The idea that these are "real" people gives psychological significance to the viewers' [understanding] of superiority—it may not matter much if the storyline is realistic, so long as the characters are ordinary people. Further, the message of reality television—that millions of people are interested in watching real life experiences of ordinary people— implies that ordinary people are important.[26]

Reiss and Wiltz also found that vengeance ranked the second highest on the list of desires that were important to reality TV viewers. They claim this makes sense because many reality shows are concerned with competitions and conflicts between participants. The study also showed that people who sought out social situations were slightly more likely to watch reality television than those who did not and that people who placed a low value on order (organization) might be turned off by all the rules that participants on reality competition shows must follow.

It is important to note that the study found no relationship between either intelligence level or physical activity and the viewing of reality programs. Both the study subjects who watched reality television and those who did not were equally motivated by curiosity (the desire for knowledge) and the desire for physical exercise. This finding conflicts with common beliefs that people who watch reality programs are of below-average intelligence and are physically inactive.

The study did reveal that the appeal of a certain show to a certain individual varies according to the desires that are more important to that individual. Reiss gives the example of *Temptation Island*, a former Fox show in which couples had their romantic and sexual loyalty to each other tested. This show was found to be more appealing to those who ranked honor as low on their scale of desires.

Steven Reiss's 16 Basic Desires Model

Motive	Intrinsic Feeling (Positive)
Acceptance: Desire for approval	Self-Confidence
Curiosity: Desire for knowledge	Wonderment
Eating: Desire for food	Satiation
Family: Desire to raise own children	Love
Honor: Desire to obey a traditional moral code; loyal to the traditional values of one's clan/ethnic group	Loyalty
Idealism: Desire to improve society (including altruism, justice)	Compassion
Independence: Desire for individuality, autonomy	Freedom
Order: Desire to organize (including desire for ritual)	Comfort
Physical Exercise: Desire to exercise muscles	Vitality
Romance: Desire for courting	Ecstasy
Power: Desire to influence (including leadership, related to mastery)	Self-Efficacy
Saving: Desire to collect	Ownership
Social Contact: Desire for peer companionship, friends (desire to play)	Fun
Status: Desire for social standing/importance (desire for attention)	Self-Importance
Tranquility: Desire for inner peace, safety (avoid anxiety, fear)	Relaxation
Vengeance: Desire to get even (including desire to win)	Vindication

Taken from: Reiss Profile Website. www.reissprofile.eu/basicdesire.

The Second Nabi Study

A second study by Nabi, along with Carmen Stitt, Jeff Halford, and Keli Finnerty, was performed after the Reiss study. The results were published in *Media Psychology* in 2006. Nabi and her colleagues built upon Nabi's 2003 research as well as that of Reiss and Wiltz. They examined whether the motivations for watching reality programs differed from those for watching fiction-based (scripted) programs and how the enjoyment of viewers of reality television differed according to the type of reality program(s) they watched.

The Osbournes

The Osbournes first aired on MTV in 2002. The show featured Ozzy Osbourne, his wife and manager Sharon, and their children Kelly and Jack. Another daughter, Aimee, refused to participate in the filming. In the second season the family also included Rob, the son of a friend of Sharon's. Rob came to live with the Osbournes after his mother passed away. Although the show was often played for laughs, it did document some serious events in the lives of the Osbournes, such as Sharon's battle with cancer.

Much of what people found appealing about the show was how it imitated a traditional family sitcom in such a funny way. Although in some respects the Osbournes were a typical family, in many ways they were not. As author David S. Escoffery notes, in the first episode of the series, when the family is moving into a new house, "We . . . see boxes labeled 'Devil Heads' and 'Dead Things' along with 'Pots and Pans' and 'Linens.'" The entire family cursed and shouted constantly, and Ozzy and Sharon's parenting skills were considered questionable

Ozzy and Sharon Osbourne starred in the reality show The Osbournes, *which played for laughs but also showed serious moments in their family life.*

by many. Yet therapists who watched and analyzed the show said the family was a close and loving one despite its odd behavior.

The final season of *The Osbournes* aired in 2005, but in 2012 it was announced that an animated version of the show, called *The F'n Osbournes*, was in the works.

David S. Escoffery. *How Real Is Reality TV?* Jefferson, NC: McFarland, 2006, p. 107.

Again, the participants of the study were residents of Tucson, Arizona, who had reported for jury duty. Half received surveys asking them about fictional programming they watched, and the other half received surveys asking about reality programming. One of the questions on both surveys asked viewers to list the emotions and reactions they tended to experience when watching the programming in question (both fictional and reality).

The study found that people did not watch reality programming to experience pleasure through voyeurism, judge others, or compare themselves to people on the shows (social comparison) any more than they did for fictional programming. For reality programming, experiencing curiosity, happiness, surprise, and relief increased enjoyment of these shows, while experiencing anger lessened it.

The study also indicated that different types of reality programs offered viewers different types of enjoyment. For example, romance-based reality programs such as *The Bachelor* were enhanced by voyeurism, whereas talent-based programs such as *American Idol* rated high in the enjoyment of judging others and of parasocial relationships. (Parasocial relationships are those in which only one of the people involved knows a great

Families enjoy watching reality shows because the shows allow them to share experiences of curiosity, happiness, surprise, and relief.

deal about the other, such as the relationship between a celebrity and a fan.) However, the strongest predictor of enjoyment across all the reality show subgroups—except for the romance subgroup—was happiness. Nabi and her colleagues concluded, "It appears that the enjoyment people [get] from watching others, that is, our [natural] curiosity about the human condition in its various forms, is an important component to the appeal and enjoyment of [reality programming] and one that distinguishes reality from fictional programming."[27] In other words, the knowledge that a show's events are real—or at least are presented as real—often leads viewers to believe they are learning and experiencing things that they would be unlikely to experience or learn from watching a scripted program.

THE "REALITY" OF REALITY TELEVISION

In this day and age, the majority of people seem aware that reality programs are very rarely completely "real." Indeed, in 2005 a survey commissioned by MSNBC found that 82 percent of those polled believed reality shows were either totally or mostly made up. This knowledge, however, does not necessarily prevent someone from enjoying a show. According to a *Pittsburgh Post-Gazette* article, "Nobody minds a goosed, amped version of the facts if it adds to entertainment pleasure, and viewers have learned how to watch reality TV with a trained suspension of disbelief. Just like, say, live theatre."[28] Nonetheless, it might be surprising to some people to learn just how much the action on reality programs might be manipulated.

Casting a Reality Show

The manipulation of a reality show begins early—when a show is being cast. Applicants for many reality programs must go through a long process that can involve making videotapes of themselves, numerous interviews, background checks, psychological testing, and even physical examinations. In most situations casting directors work to fill certain "roles" and to find a particular mix of personalities. Shows commonly seek out cast members that fit certain stereotypes or categories, such as the "bad boy" or the "party girl." The ethnicity, race, gender, and sexual orientation of possible participants are taken into consideration for shows that want to have diverse cast members. Casting directors are not alone, however, in the effort to fill roles with interesting characters. Often the contestants themselves

Models wait to audition for Australia's Next Top Model. *Applicants for reality shows must go through a long process that can involve videotaping, numerous interviews, background checks, psychological testing, and physical examinations.*

have learned how to play the game to attract the interest of the producers. Numerous resources exist that reality show hopefuls can consult for auditioning tips, including websites, books, and even classes and workshops at places such as the New York Reality TV School. The notion that cast members are "real" people just looking to be themselves is sometimes hard to believe.

Psychological testing can help the producers make sure they can provide a balanced and interesting show. An interview with

Richard Levak, a psychologist who has worked on programs such as *Survivor* and *The Apprentice*, revealed:

> If you put 16 conflict-avoiders together on an island . . . you won't end up with very interesting TV. On the other hand, if you compose a group entirely with aggressive, [outgoing] Type A personalities, you may produce some fireworks, but it's unlikely you'll [keep] an audience's attention over weeks. Instead, the most compelling viewing comes when people with different yet recognizable personalities evolve over time in relation to those around them while dealing with competition and [difficult] circumstances.[29]

Psychological exams can also give producers a clue about how a show's participant will react to a situation or challenge. This can mean there will be fewer surprises that the producers will have to deal with once filming begins.

SCREENING OF POTENTIAL CAST MEMBERS

"There's a drug test, STD [sexually transmitted disease] test, psych profiles, background checks. It's probably easier to get a government job than it is to get on this show. I know people think we go out and find crazies, but that's not the case."—Chris Harrison, host of *The Bachelor*.

Quoted in Jessica Shaw. "*Bachelor* Questions Answered." *Entertainment Weekly*, March 9, 2012, p. 17.

After the casting is complete, participants are required to sign very long contracts, some of which give reality show producers the right to make up anything they like about the cast member. For example, as noted by Christopher Bell in *American Idolatry*, the *Idol* contract plainly states, "I hereby grant the Producer the unconditional right throughout the universe [forever] to use, simulate, or portray my name, likeness, voice, singing voice, personality, personal identification or personal experiences, my life story, biographical data, incidents, situations, events which heretofore occurred or hereafter occur."[30] Bell points out that the use of the word "simulate" gives the producer the legal right to reproduce the contestant's likeness or voice in any way he or she chooses, even if the contestant objects. Similarly, a section of the *Real World* contract reads: "Producer may depict, portray me and my Life Story either accurately or with such liberties and modifications as Producer determines necessary or desirable in its sole discretion for the purposes of fictionalization, dramatization, or other purposes . . . and by means of actors who may or may not resemble me."[31] In other words, the producer can make up anything he or she likes about cast members and even stage scenes involving them when they are not present. Contracts such as these mean that viewers might wish to pay attention to the old saying "Believe none of what you hear and half of what you see."

Are Reality Show Cast Members Being "Real?"

Once the cast of a reality program has been set and filming begins, the participants may or may not be showing their real personalities in front of the cameras. Several memorable reality show participants, such as *Survivor*'s Richard Hatch and *The Apprentice*'s Omarosa Manigault-Stallworth, said after their seasons were over that they were very aware of the cameras and were playing to them. Manigault-Stallworth, who is one of reality television's best-known villains, told one reporter that she had followed the advice of a friend who said, "The fabric of reality TV is conflict, so make sure that you're either in the fight, breaking the fight up, or starting the fight."[32] Likewise, Hatch claimed that viewers saw his "game face" and not his real personality during *Survivor*.

It is not only those competing in reality show contests that have admitted to changing their behavior in order to be more entertaining. Paris Hilton has said she played up her "ditzy blonde" act on *The Simple Life*, in which she and fellow socialite Nicole Ritchie left the big city to live on a farm. "I'm doing a TV show," she said. "Obviously I wouldn't act like that in real life. The things I do on the show, I know I'm being filmed. . . . It makes people laugh. That's all I care about. I'm just entertaining people."[33] Tyra Banks, the host and a judge on *America's Next*

Mark Burnett

Mark Burnett is a producer of well-known reality television shows in many countries. Some of the shows he has produced in the United States include *Survivor*, *The Voice*, *The Apprentice*, *Celebrity Apprentice*, and *Are You Smarter than a Fifth-Grader?*

Burnett was born in London, England, in 1960, to working-class parents. At seventeen he joined the British army and served active duty in Northern Ireland and the Falkland Islands. At the end of his service, Burnett accepted a position as a military adviser for the British in Central America. However, when he stopped over in Los Angeles on his way to Central America in 1982, Burnett decided to stay in the United States. He soon found work as a nanny.

One of Burnett's employers eventually employed him to sell insurance. Burnett then went from selling insurance to selling T-shirts to starting a marketing and advertising firm. Not long after this, he became interested in a French competition show called *Raid Gauloises*, in which teams competed in exotic locations. Burnett put together an American team and took part in several "raids." Once he felt that he fully understood the game, he created a similar competition for American television and called it *Eco-Challenge*. *Eco-Challenge* was first broadcast on MTV in the mid-1990s. In 1998 Burnett purchased the rights to *Survivor* and brought it to America, helping usher in the current era of reality programming in the country.

Mark Burnett, standing, far right, and the cast of The Voice. *Burnett has produced several hit reality shows.*

Top Model, explained in 2011 that she created a confident, bold, pushy character for the show and that in real life she is shy and insecure.

It is possible that these claims are just a way for people to try to improve their image if they seemed mean or stupid on a show. However, in some cases, other participants on a program have agreed that their fellow cast members acted differently on camera. According to Derek Woodruff, a contestant on Logo's florists' competition *The Arrangement*, "Personally, I know that I was true to myself on and off camera, but *I know for a fact* that some of the other contestants put on their stage face for the camera, because in person, they were not like that at all."[34]

Despite all this, show producers claim that what the viewer sees is ultimately the real thing, especially in the case of shows like *Big Brother* or *The Real World*, which feature constant monitoring of the cast members. Mary-Ellis Bunim, cocreator of *Real World* and *Road Rules*, once insisted, "You can't sustain a character that isn't true to yourself day and night, for thirteen weeks. It's just not possible. It would drive you mad."[35] Some cast members agree, such as Burton Roberts, who appeared on the third season of *Survivor*. At the time he submitted an audition for the show, Roberts was a former Eagle Scout who had already participated in other outdoor challenges—a perfect fit for the show. According to Roberts, "My strategy in the first week was to lay low, to not stand out, and to try not to be a leader under any circumstances. That lasted a whole six hours. . . . At the end of the day, you're pretty much who you are, and that will come out."[36] Former *Apprentice* contestant Sam Solovey has a slightly different perspective: "People accused me of playing to the cameras, but I don't think I did. I think the cameras draw the extremes of your personality out. If you're shy, the cameras make you more shy. If you're someone who loves an audience, they push you in that direction."[37]

However, some producers, including Bunim's former creative partner Jonathan Murray, have admitted that their shows have become harder to cast, partly because young people raised on reality television now come in knowing which "character" they want to play on the show. Murray stresses that what producers really want are honest, complex personalities who have not figured out their lives yet, not those who seek to be on a reality show to become famous or start acting careers. As a result, some producers, such as Thom Beers of *Deadliest Catch* and *Storage Wars*, search for cast members in ways other than casting calls or audition tapes. Beers claims he likes to find people through friends of friends or from messages he sees on Facebook or Craigslist, because, as he puts it, "Normal people aren't necessarily there looking for fame but more likely looking for a slightly used mattress."[38] Beers also says he is not above firing a cast member if he feels that person is acting fake in front of the camera.

Producer Manipulation

Cast members looking for fame—or used furniture—are not the only issue that affect the filming of a reality show. There are many ways that producers might manipulate a show. Producers control everything from the environment in which the contestants are placed to what eventually ends up being shown on the air.

Stirring Up Conflict

"The producers have a big role in what's happening on the show. They create a lot of drama and they start a lot of the fights . . . they will say so and so said this about you behind your back, and she said she slept with your boyfriend. It's like high school."—Jayde Nicole, cast member on *The Hills* and *Holly's World*.

Quoted in Andrea Canning and Elizabeth Stuart. "Reality Show Violence Getting Too Real?" ABC News, March 30, 2011. http://abcnews.go.com/Entertainment/reality-tv-show-violence-real-life-consequences-teen/story?id=13256971.

Participants on reality shows often have interesting things to say about their experiences once a show has ended. Some have claimed that producers used various methods to influence their behavior on camera. As many reality cast members are not represented by a labor union, they do not have the same protections and rights given to actors on scripted shows. This means that producers can legally treat them in ways that might endanger their physical and mental health. Participants on *Project Runway* and *Hell's Kitchen* have said they were almost completely shut off from the outside world and only allowed a few hours of sleep every night. This left them stressed and too sleepy to function well. In some cases alcohol has been provided in order to fire up the behavior of cast members. One *New York Times* article reported that "during the 2006 season of the popular ABC dating show *The Bachelor*, the contestants waited in vans for several hours while the crew set up for a 12-hour 'arrival' party where, two contestants said, there was little food but bottomless glasses of wine. When producers judged the [action] too boring, they sent out a production assistant with a tray of shots."[39]

Kristin Cavallari (with microphone), one of the stars of MTV's reality show The Hills, *admitted that a large part of the program's final season was scripted.*

If producers cannot incite the drama they want by keeping cast members tired and giving them alcohol, they might become even more directly involved. In an interview, one *Bachelor* producer revealed:

> Well, in the private one-on-one interviews with a producer (like me) it is [my] job to get the [trash talk] started, like "tell me honestly what you think of Sally"—if the interviewee does not want to respond in a catty way then the producer will usually go to the next level, like "well I personally think she is a self absorbed, attention starved skank," and then see if the person will take the bait. Once you start learning who in the house is not well liked it is easy to start seeding conversations and gossip.[40]

The producer also admitted that food or rewards were sometimes withheld from contestants unless the contestants gave them the type of comments they wanted.

Editing, Scripting, and Other Tricks of the Trade

If all this still does not get the results the producers hope for, they can simply edit footage of the cast members to have it say or show whatever they like. One editing method is known as "Frankenbiting." In this process, bits and pieces of audio commentary by a cast member are spliced (joined) together to create a new sentence that may be completely contrary to what the person originally said. *Time* magazine gives an example of this that occurred on ABC's *The Dating Game*. According to the article, one of the female cast members did not like the male cast member the producers wanted her to like. So when the crew was taping an interview with the woman, they asked who her favorite celebrity was. She responded that she really loved Adam Sandler. Later, the editor spliced out Sandler's name and replaced it with audio of the woman saying the male cast member's name.

Editing tricks can be visual as well. In the same *Time* article, Jeff Bartsch, a freelance reality show editor, said that scenes are sometimes shown out of order or context (the set of details or facts that surround a particular event) to add more drama. He mentioned the show *Blind Date* and explained how the editing in one episode made it appear that a male participant was having a bad time on his date by showing scenes of him looking bored and unfocused while the woman was talking. In reality, those shots of him had been filmed while his date was in the restroom. Many reality show cast members throughout the years have complained about such editing, saying that the producers spliced footage in ways that made them look like villains. Although it is difficult to argue with this when it comes to examples such as the one on *Blind Date*, other times the producers insist they are simply working with what they are given by the cast members. In the words of one producer, "If you did it and it got caught on film, it doesn't matter how much other delightful stuff you did—you can't blame the editors for using the good stuff, and you can't claim they [made it up]."[41] Another producer, Mark Cronin, explains that it is very hard to do what he calls "editing uphill" and tell a story that did not happen. He says that once a producer starts changing the basic truth of, for example, a relationship between two people, the producer then has to be aware of *all* the interactions between those two people for the rest of the show. He or she will have to continue to edit these interactions so they continue to support the fake story the producer has created. Cronin claims that all this trouble is generally not worth the effort to producers, so they are unlikely to make major changes to a storyline.

SEARCHING FOR DRAMA

"I'm not an industry insider, but I can't imagine that production teams would want to exclude people with . . . personality disorders, because they make for such good television."
—Psychotherapist Nathan Gehlert.

Quoted in Liane Bonin Starr. "Do You Have to Be Crazy to Be a Reality TV Star?" *Starr Raving* (blog), HitFix, September 1, 2011. www.hitfix.com/blogs/starr-raving/posts/do-you-have-to-be-crazy-to-be-a-reality-tv-star.

Some shows do not have to be heavily edited after filming, because they are partially scripted to begin with. In 2004 a reporter for the *Los Angeles Times* revealed a nineteen-page outline for an episode of *Queer Eye for the Straight Guy* that even included scripted lines for the straight guy to say. When *Jersey Shore* was filming in Italy in 2011, several locals and extras reported seeing rehearsals of scenes, as well as reshoots from different camera angles with the cast members repeating the same dialogue over and over. Also in 2011, Kristin Cavallari, one of the stars of the popular MTV show *The Hills*, admitted what fans had suspected for a long time—that a large part of the program's final season was scripted.

Producers can even manipulate the outcome of competition shows—or at least they can try. During one season of *Big Brother*, the producers felt the cast was not interesting enough and the show was losing viewers. They offered to pay fifty thousand dollars to any Houseguest willing to leave and be replaced by a more exciting personality. (No one volunteered.) Critics have accused producers of shows such as *Dancing with the Stars* of manipulating outcomes by ranking certain desirable contestants in the "bottom three" to mobilize their fan bases to vote for them, even though those contestants might not have actually been among the lowest vote getters. On *Idol*, fans for years have accused the producers of lining up their favorite contestants in the last spot—the so-called pimp spot—on performance nights so they will be fresher in the minds of voters. The producers, however, deny this, claiming that performance order is based on factors such as alternating genders and the best arrangement of songs.

Are Reality Contests Rigged?

Issues such as these, of course, raise the issue of competition rigging, or manipulating a contest so that the producers' choice wins. Such claims are hardly new to reality television. In the 1950s the industry was rocked by quiz show scandals that involved several programs, including three of the most popular contests at the time, *The $64,000 Question*, *Dotto*, and *Twenty-One*. Those scandals resulted in amendments to the Communications Act of 1934 that made it a crime to rig contests—but only contests of "intellectual knowledge or intellectual skill," such as traditional game shows. Reality show competitions do not appear to be included in the law's scope. Most shows have reserved the right to change the process of crowning a winner at will—for example, the website for *So You Think You Can Dance* frankly states: "Rules and procedures are subject to change at producers' discretion without notice."[42]

The producers, however, insist that this is simply a safety measure in case something goes wrong with the call-in voting system. According to Nigel Lythgoe, producer of both *Idol* and *Dance*, "Whenever you do a contract, you have to anticipate every angle, because you can't tell what's going to happen." He also insisted that rigging a contest would be a foolish move, saying, "The minute you take away somebody the public's voting for, you're screwing with the program. . . . There's no logic to [interfering]."[43]

COMPETITIONS HARD TO MANIPULATE

"Every year, fans of *Dancing with the Stars* threaten to boycott the show because they feel ABC manipulated the votes and the wrong D-level dancer won. Despite this, viewers still show up . . . because when it's said and done, there aren't producers out there manipulating Steve-O's legs while he's fox-trotting. He's doing it all himself."—Lynette Rice of *Entertainment Weekly*.

Quoted in Michael Ventre. "Just How Real Are Reality TV Shows?" *Today*, April 14, 2009. http://today.msnbc.msn.com/id/30092600/ns/today-entertainment/t/just-how-real-are-reality-tv-shows.

And yet accusations continue. After the current wave of reality programming began in the early 2000s, one of the first charges of vote rigging involved *Survivor*. In 2001 a former contestant, Stacey Stillman, filed a lawsuit against CBS and the show's producer, Mark Burnett, claiming that Burnett told two other contestants to vote her off the show. Burnett and CBS in return sued Stillman for $5 million for harming the show's reputation and breaking her contract. They claimed, in part, that she had broken the eighty-three-page confidentiality agreement she had signed before the show began filming. (Confidentiality agreements, which almost all reality show cast members must sign,

How Much Money Do Reality Show Participants Make?

How much money someone earns for participating in a reality show varies greatly from show to show. Although typically the producers try to keep salaries secret, once the shows have aired, cast members sometimes reveal how much they were paid. At other times, media sources manage to find out on their own. Reality shows often pay participants very little compared to actors on scripted shows. For example, it has been reported that contestants on *Big Brother* earn only $750 per week. *Survivor* participants are supposedly paid based on how long they remain on the show; the first person voted off is paid $2,500, the sixth person voted off is paid $10,000, and so forth.

On the other end of the range, people who have become famous by appearing on a reality show are often paid much more. Bethenny Frankel of *The Real Housewives of New York City* reportedly made between $30,000 to $40,000 per episode while she was on the show. The cast members of *Jersey Shore* are said to make $100,000 per episode. Celebrities who appear on reality shows make even more: Christina Aguilera makes $225,000 per episode to be a coach on *The Voice*, and insiders say Jennifer Lopez was paid close to $20 million to judge *American Idol*'s eleventh season.

say that a cast member cannot reveal certain things about the filming of a show until a set amount of time has passed.) The case was eventually settled out of court.

Charges that *American Idol* is rigged in some fashion arise almost every season. One notable example occurred in 2008 when judge Paula Abdul gave her comments on contestant Jason Castro's song before he actually performed it. This led some to suspect that the judges' comments are set before they even see the performances or are fed to them by the show's producers. A year later, semifinalist Ju'Not Joyner claimed he was booted from the competition over concerns he had about the contract that he was required to sign and because he would not let the show use his personal life to gain viewer sympathy. In an online chat with *Idol* fans, Joyner claimed, "It's a fixed thing if I ever saw one. . . . The producers know who they want and they slant it to reflect that. They fix it in a way that makes you surprised but it's still manipulated. . . . Do you think a billion-dollar enterprise is subject to the whim of the public?"[44]

Dancing with the Stars has also been accused of rigging outcomes on several occasions. The show's formula of combining audience votes with the judges' scores to identify the lowest vote getter makes for a less clear-cut result than those shows that sim-

Survivor contestant Stacey Stillman sued the show's producer, Mark Burnett, claiming he had told other contestants to vote her off the show. He countersued and the case was eventually settled out of court.

ply tally viewers' votes. Many viewers could not figure out how poor-performing contestants such as former star of *Jon and Kate Plus Eight* Kate Gosselin and Bristol Palin, the daughter of vice presidential nominee Sarah Palin, remained in the competition week after week, and they expressed anger when more talented dancers were sent home. (In one infamous incident, a Wyoming man was so upset by Palin's bad dancing that he shot his television set and had a fifteen-hour standoff with police.) Executive producer Conrad Green defended the show against claims that its voting system had to be at fault after Palin made it to the finals of the show's eleventh season. He stated that the voting was overseen by the Broadcast Standards Team, which operates on its own with no input or influence from the show or network. He also defended the program's special voting formula, saying, "Everyone is having a go at our system, but unlike *American Idol*, our professional judges count for half of the total for each couple, so there's already a built-in attempt to make the dance quality matter. . . . I think it's absolutely fair."[45]

Are Voting Systems Reliable?

Claims of vote rigging often concern the call-in systems that the programs use to collect viewer votes. ABC did admit that its online and telephone voting system was swamped by a record amount of traffic one week during the Palin season. However, ABC insisted that all three finalists were affected equally and that the problem was quickly corrected. The amount of time allowed for people to cast votes was not extended despite the problem, however, and some people may have run out of time before they were able to place a vote again. Others might simply have given up after their first attempt was unsuccessful. This did not help matters for ABC in a season already full of viewer complaints.

Other claims of call-in system issues affecting competition outcomes have involved *Idol*. In the show's first season, it was reported that members of a group of about one hundred phone hackers with high-tech tools had targeted the show. These hackers were able to place ten thousand votes per night from a single phone line with a single phone call. *Idol*'s production company insisted that these calls still represented such a small number of total votes that they did not change the season's outcome. The *Idol* staff now looks at the calls coming in to identify such instances of power dialing.

In other cases incorrect phone numbers have been displayed on-screen for contestants. When this happened in 2005, *Idol* producers were forced to throw out all votes received that night and rebroadcast the show the following day. Another technical mistake occurred the following season when some callers dialing in for popular *Idol* contestant Chris Daughtry were surprised to hear fellow contestant Katharine McPhee's message thanking them for their votes. Daughtry was eliminated the following night, and many of his fans blamed the call-in error. In 2006 *Rock Star Supernova* also dealt with technical difficulties when viewers complained that the online voting system was not working properly for about an hour after the show ended.

Controversy swirled around American Idol *in 2005 when contestant Chris Daughtry (pictured) was eliminated after a night during which the call-in voting system experienced problems.*

During the 2009 season of American Idol *fans of finalist Adam Lambert (shown) were angry over viewers' power-texting multiple votes at once for the other finalist, Kris Allen. The show's producers claimed that the number of such votes was so small that it did not affect the outcome.*

Another controversy occurred in 2009 during the season eight finale of *Idol*. AT&T, one of the show's sponsors, handed out phones to fans at parties held in Arkansas for finalist (and eventual winner) Kris Allen. The AT&T employees also offered the attendees tips about how to text votes and how to power text multiple votes at once, even though power texting is against the show's rules. Fans of the other finalist, Adam Lambert, were angry and demanded that Fox address the issue. However, just as in the first-season hacking scandal, the show's producers claimed the votes represented such a small portion of the total that they did not affect the outcome. AT&T offered a statement of apology, claiming its workers were "caught up in the enthusiasm of rooting for their hometown contestant. . . . Going forward we will make sure our employees understand our sponsorship celebrates the competition, not individual contestants."[46]

In the end, then, although the voting systems are imperfect and vulnerable to technical issues, producers do not believe those issues have ever changed the final outcome of a show.

CHAPTER 4

Is Reality Television Harmful to Society?

Complaints about the amount of "reality" that is actually a part of reality television is not the only issue the genre has to contend with. Reality television has the worst reputation of any type of television programming. It has been accused of everything from causing mean-spirited behavior to encouraging teens to get pregnant just so they can be on television. Parents' organizations speak out against reality TV and claim it is destroying the morals of today's children and teens. They worry that young people will imitate the cast members on some of the shows and think that it is okay to get drunk, do drugs, or sleep around. Others point out that this same behavior can also be found on scripted shows and say it is unfair to place so much of the blame on reality television. As an article in *Time* explains, "When a reality show [presents] bad behavior, it's immoral, [anti-women], sexist or sick. When [crime-family drama] *The Sopranos* does the same thing, it's [good] storytelling."[47] The article goes on to say that people assume that viewers of *The Sopranos* are able to separate fact from fiction more easily than fans of reality programs because *Sopranos* viewers are more intelligent. Experts believe this is not true. So where does the truth lie? Is reality television harming society?

Violence in Reality Television

One major criticism aimed at reality television is that it contains too much violence. In the last few years, many media scholars have noted an increase in incidents of physical violence on reality shows. In an episode of *Jersey Shore*, Mike "The Situation" Sorrentino slapped fellow cast member Snooki in the face and called it a "love tap." On an episode of *Kourtney & Khloe Take Miami*, Kourtney Kardashian's boyfriend Scott Disick drank too much and went on a rampage, breaking bottles and punching walls. A frightened Kardashian locked herself and their infant son in another room. In 2010 Amber Portwood of MTV's *Teen Mom* was shown kicking, punching, and slapping the father of her child.

Some worry that if young people look to reality stars as role models, they might imitate the violence committed by the stars. Others suggest that viewers might come to expect that bad behavior will be rewarded with fame and fortune, which could influence their own choices. According to psychologist Stacey Kaiser, "Things that we used to look away from are things that we watch on television on a daily basis. . . . It sends a message to viewers that it's something that's socially acceptable to our society these days."[48]

Defenders of reality shows say that when reality shows present bad behavior it is called immoral, sexist, or sick but that when violent dramas like The Sopranos *(shown) do the same thing it is called powerful storytelling.*

In an episode of Jersey Shore, *Mike Sorrentino, left, slapped fellow cast member Snooki, right, and called it a "love tap." Other reality shows have had similar incidents of violence.*

Others, however, argue that airing the violence that occurs on reality shows actually has some benefits. Jenny Salisbury, development director of the domestic violence organization A Woman's Place, says it can be a good thing if it helps people become aware of the problems that violence creates. As she explains, "By not showing or making the audience aware that the incident did occur, the media would be ignoring the issue as opposed to responding to it. Domestic violence is an issue that affects everybody and needs to be brought to the forefront."[49]

Some networks seem to accept this responsibility—during the *Teen Mom* episode that involved Portwood hitting her boyfriend, MTV did air a domestic violence public service announcement during the commercial breaks.

While physical violence may be on the rise in reality shows, scripted programming displays even more of this type of aggression. A study performed by researchers at Brigham Young University found that scripted programs contained more verbal aggression as well. (The researchers defined verbal aggression as using words to hurt another person, such as calling them names or insulting them.) However, they found that reality programs feature much more relational aggression. In this type of aggression, a person seeks to harm another person's social standing or relationships with other people. Examples are gossiping, spreading rumors, or keeping people out of a certain social circle. The researchers discovered that this type of behavior is displayed more commonly by females on reality programs, which helps add to the stereotype of the "mean girl."

ONE PRODUCER'S VIEWPOINT

"We have no obligation to make history; we have no obligation to make art; we have no obligation to make a statement; to make money is our only objective."—Michael Eisner, former CEO of the Walt Disney Company.

Quoted in Laurie Ouellette and James Hay. *Better Living Through Reality Television.* New York: Blackwell, 2008, p. 34.

Are the instances of verbal and relational aggression shown on reality programs affecting the behaviors and beliefs of the young people who watch them? A recent survey by the Girl Scouts Research Institute that attempted to answer this question had mixed results. The survey was given to 1,141 girls aged eleven to seventeen who reported watching reality TV. Eighty-six percent of them thought that reality shows want to make girls argue with each other to make the show more exciting. Seventy-three percent said reality shows try to make people think that fighting is a normal part of a romantic relationship. And 70 percent thought that reality shows try to make people think it is okay to treat others badly. Some experts see these results as promising because they suggest that girls are aware that the shows are deliberately working to influence the behavior of the participants and that reality programs may be giving a false view of what normal behavior is.

AN OBLIGATION TO THE VIEWING PUBLIC?

"If a production company creates a show with the . . . intention of trying to make money from the humiliation and suffering which they themselves create for unsuspecting people, then that seems to me to be immoral and unconscionable."—Lecturer Austin Cline.

Austin Cline. "Ethics and Reality TV: Should We Really Watch?" About.com. http://athe ism.about.com/library/FAQs/phil/blphil_eth_realitytv.htm.

On the other hand, the survey also showed that 37 percent of those who watched a lot of reality television said that being mean earns a person more respect than being nice. And 28 percent said a person has to be mean to others to get what he or she wants. This suggests that, despite being aware that the reality programs are seeking to influence them, the girls may still be incorporating the negative behavior seen on some of those shows into their behavior.

Does This TV Show Make Me Look Fat?

Self-image is also a concern. Another section of the Girl Scouts study asked girls who watched reality shows to answer questions about self-image, including physical appearance. This is because another criticism of reality television is that certain reality programs might cause people to feel bad about how they look. Judith Orloff, a professor of psychiatry at University of California–Los Angeles (UCLA), said of shows such as *The Real Housewives* franchise, "These shows can . . . be very destructive if younger people watch them. They're getting the message,

'You'll be happy if you . . . get a nose job or a face lift.' That's all false. Those messages cause girls to become anorexic and boys to feel horrible about themselves."[50] A third of the girls in the Girl Scouts survey said they believed a girl's value is based on how she looks, and 28 percent said they would rather be recognized for being pretty than having a good personality.

A study published by Charlotte and Patrick Markey in the academic journal *Body Image* in 2010 found that watching reality television seemed to play a major role in convincing young people to get cosmetic, or plastic, surgery. The researchers polled two hundred men and women with an average age of twenty about their reactions to shows that focus on body makeovers. The study found that the women were more likely to consider plastic surgery than the men. It also found that those who watched makeover shows were more likely to consider getting plastic surgery than those who watched other shows. According to the American Society of Plastic Surgeons, although adults tend to get plastic surgery in order to stand out from others, young people tend to want to get rid of certain physical characteristics so they will look *more* like their

Critics say that shows like The Real Housewives of Orange County *(shown) send messages such as, "You can be happy if you just get a nose job or face-lift." Such messages may prompt girls to become anorexic and boys to feel bad about themselves.*

peers. The article in *Body Image* states that there is no definite proof that plastic surgery makes people happier. Nevertheless, there are people who appeared on body-altering shows who say they are glad they did and that their lives have changed for the better.

Weight-loss shows are generally less controversial than those that focus on cosmetic surgery. The goal of increasing someone's health by reducing obesity is less objectionable than changing someone's physical appearance to increase their attraction. However, although weight loss itself may be a good idea, health experts sometimes criticize the way the participants lose weight on reality television. They claim that losing so much weight so quickly may result in heart problems or loss of bone density and that, in some cases, the emotional issues that have caused participants to overeat in the first place are not addressed by the show. These experts also worry that people at home do not have the same access to medical supervision as the participants and could harm themselves if they try to follow the routines shown on these programs.

Other experts, however, disagree. They think the shows may exert a positive influence on overweight viewers. Seeing people triumph on these shows might inspire obese viewers to lose weight and regain their own health and energy. Lorette Lavine, a nurse and social worker who treats obese people, says, "On *The Biggest Loser*, the trainers seem to be really involved with the contestants on the show. They have a huge team and are quite clear that it is not just about dieting but also about maintaining a healthful lifestyle and educating people. They push them to exercise. They work with chefs skilled in healthful cooking. They try to get them to reach their maximum health potential."[51] She also points out that many of the contestants have other health issues, such as diabetes and high blood pressure, that improve as they move through the program.

Treatment of Women in Reality Programming

The portrayal of women is another of the many issues raised about reality television. Many critics agree that women are often made

Reality TV: A Danger to Human Welfare?

In 2010 a camera crew was filming a police raid in Detroit for A&E's *The First 48*, a program that follows homicide detectives as they attempt to solve murders. During the raid, police threw a flash grenade into the house to stun those inside. Moments later a gun went off, killing seven-year-old Aiyana Stanley-Jones.

After the girl's death, her family sued the city, the police, and also A&E, claiming that the fact that the raid was being videotaped for the show caused police to act in a more aggressive manner than they normally would have. An attorney who represented the family claimed that the police were excited to be on camera and were showing off. The Detroit police denied this. One officer said that he thought the presence of cameras actually acted to restrain the police from taking any questionable actions, since they knew they were being filmed.

After the shooting, Detroit's mayor passed a law that said camera crews could no longer ride along with police. The officer who shot Aiyana was charged with involuntary manslaughter and reckless use of a firearm. One of the *First 48* producers was charged with perjury (lying in court) and obstruction of justice. Their trials were set for 2013.

Krystal Sanders holds a picture of her seven-year-old niece, Aiyana Stanley-Jones, accidentally killed by a Detroit policeman during filming of the reality show The First 48.

to look catty, jealous, desperate, and stupid on reality shows—particularly in romantic dating shows such as *The Bachelor*. According to Jennifer L. Pozner in *Reality Bites Back*:

> Reality TV women are [shamed] in any number of ways. They cry in limos after being kicked to the curb. They [panic] when the guy they've known for, oh, three hours says he doesn't see forever in their future. They abandon their belief systems to suit their men: For example, a vegetarian described eating meat for the first time in twelve years just because [the Bachelor] fed it to her. "My stomach will probably never be the same, but at least I touched his hand," she said, grateful for crumbs.[52]

The women on these shows are often seen making nasty comments and talking behind the backs of their fellow female participants as well. "Catfights" between women are played to their fullest dramatic potential.

Women are also sometimes portrayed as less intelligent or capable than men. Pozner points to an example of this in *The Real Housewives of Atlanta*, when one of the wives was shown trying to help her nine-year-old child with his math homework. She was unable to do basic algebra and had to turn to her husband for help. Another woman on the same show was apparently unable to spell the word "cat." On the twentieth season of *The Amazing Race*, which is generally considered one of the more "respectable" reality shows, contestant Rachel, while trying to help her male partner set up a solar panel, comments, "I'm sorry I'm not good at this. I'm sorry I'm just a girl."[53]

However, strong, capable women are also depicted on reality programs. Another episode of the same season of *The Amazing Race* featured a physical contest between two teams—one all male, one male-female—to see which could stack hay bales faster. The woman on the mixed team did the actual stacking, leading her team to victory, prompting the all-male team to pout and claim that they were "beat by a frickin' girl."[54] On programs such as *Police Women of Broward County*, women bravely serve and protect their communities. Similarly, *The First 48* often features female homicide cops who use their intelligence and skills to lead murder investigations. On the History Channel's *Swamp People*, teams compete to kill the most alligators in the Louisiana bayou. In one episode the sole female hunting duo, Liz and Kristi, bag the biggest alligator, a half-ton monster, and manage to haul it into their boat with sheer physical strength. In another episode Liz's male cousin asks the women for help with an alligator that is coming too close to his property. Liz and Kristi are portrayed as physically fit, competent women who can manage just as well as the men in a dangerous environment.

Stereotypes on Reality Programs

Women are not the only ones who are sometimes portrayed negatively on reality shows. At times stereotypes of African Americans and people of other races are used to entertain viewers. According to the *Daily Beast*, "From Oxygen's *Bad Girls* to Bravo's *Real Housewives* franchise, the small screen is awash with black females who roll their eyes, bob their heads, snap their fingers, talk trash, and otherwise reinforce the ugly stereotype of the 'angry black woman.'"[55] Some criticize the way that black men are portrayed as angry, violent, lazy, or stupid. Stereotypical Asians are usually smart, and stereotypical Latina women constantly search for sex. Producers of shows such as *The Real World* and *Big Brother*, however, defend their programs by saying that they address, rather than avoid, racial issues in ways other shows do not and break down barriers by having people of different races living and working closely together. And some nonwhite cast members have complained that it is unfair to expect them to represent their entire race.

RACISM IN REALITY PROGRAMS

"While so many Americans naively believe that we are a nation that has overcome segregation, prejudice, and racism, we still tune in to watch television shows that are full of the same damaging stereotypes that hold back entire groups of people from the equal opportunity to create their own unique and personal identities."—Social media specialist Lindsay Gulisano.

Lindsay Gulisano. "Cultivation Theory: Creating Perceptions of Life from Reality Television." University of Colorado. www.colorado.edu/communication/meta-discourses /Papers/App_Papers/Gulisano.htm.

Stereotypes are not the only racial issues in reality programming. African Americans and other races are often underrepresented on romance reality shows: There has never been a black, Latino, or Asian Bachelor or Bachelorette, and very few of the contestants on those shows are anything other than white. Some believe this is because the producers want to avoid tampering with the series' winning formula and fear how people might react to an interracial romance. The creator of these shows, however, claims this is not true: "We always want to cast for racial diversity," he claims. "It's just that for whatever reason, they don't come forward. I wish they would."[56] In 2012 at least two black men *did* attend a *Bachelor* casting event; however, those men filed a lawsuit against the show after they were not chosen. Their lawsuit argued that they were never seriously considered for casting due to their race. Cable shows such as VH1's

The racially diverse cast of MTV's The Real World *pose during a reunion. The producers claim that the show addresses racial issues in ways that no other shows do.*

Flavor of Love and *I Love New York* have featured a black main love interest and a greater number of nonwhite contestants, but those shows were also targeted for supporting racist stereotypes. VH1's executive Michael Hirschorn responded to this criticism by pointing out that the shows were more popular with black viewers than white.

REALITY TV AS A TEACHING TOOL FOR RACIAL ISSUES

"I think [reality television] offers an opportunity for parents and adults working with youth to use these types of programs as a jumping off point to talk about race and racism. I think . . . a dose of reality would help bring these issues to the surface."— Anastasia Goodstein, director of digital programs at Inspire USA Foundation.

Anastasia Goodstein. "The 'Reality' of Race in America." *Huffington Post*, January 5, 2007. www.huffingtonpost.com/anastasia-goodstein/the-reality-of-race-in-am_b_37922.html.

Other minority groups have made more noticeable progress at being included and portrayed fairly on reality programs. For example, the treatment of lesbians, gays, bisexuals, and transgenders (LGBTs) has come a long way since *An American Family*'s Lance Loud became the first openly gay person on television. Early reality shows involving gays were often not promising in terms of the treatment of their participants. In Bravo's *Boy Meets Boy*, a gay bachelor believed he was looking for a mate from among a group of other gay men but was unaware that half the men were straight and seeking to fool him. And Fox's *Playing It Straight* featured a woman who had to guess whether her male suitors were gay or straight based on their behavior—whether or not they "acted gay."

Fortunately for the gay community, *Queer Eye for the Straight Guy* premiered at around the same time as both of these shows. *Queer Eye* became very popular and helped people become more comfortable with seeing openly gay people on television. Since then many television shows that focus on gays and lesbians have

Cast members of the reality show Queer Eye for the Straight Guy *pose with fans in Las Vegas. A ratings winner,* Queer Eye *helped many people become more comfortable with seeing openly gay persons on television.*

hit the airwaves, including *Flipping Out*, *The A-List*, *Girls Who Like Boys*, *RuPaul's Drag Race*, and *The Real L Word*. Contestants on many reality competition shows, such as *Project Runway* and *The Voice*, are openly gay. *America's Next Top Model* featured a transgendered contestant, as did *The Real World: Brooklyn*. And recently the Miss Universe pageant announced it was changing its policy to allow transgendered women to compete.

Children on Reality Shows

While ethnic groups and the LGBT community worry about how they are portrayed on reality shows, the presence of other groups such as children raise other important issues. According to Child AbuseWatch, children on reality shows are considered "participants" rather than "actors," so they are not protected by child labor laws in the same way that children who appear in scripted shows are. The parents are expected to oversee their children's welfare and decide whether or not they should participate. Children—especially the younger ones—often have no say in the matter. Many people worry that children might be damaged, either physically or mentally, from participation on a reality show.

In 2007 CBS aired a program called *Kid Nation*. In the show, forty children aged eight to fifteen were placed in a ghost town in the New Mexico desert and challenged to set up their own society with no help from adults. Many critics of the show were concerned about the safety and welfare of the children, especially since they were performing numerous physical tasks. One participant's mother filed a complaint after she said her daughter was burned by grease while cooking a meal, and two other children drank bleach from an unmarked container. After hearing reports that the children were working fourteen-hour days, the state of New Mexico also charged the program with violating child labor laws. Neither lawsuit was successful, however. CBS claimed the children were never in any real danger, as paramedics, a pediatrician, an animal safety expert, and a psychologist were all available on the set.

There is concern that shows like Hoarders *(shown), which focus on real people with emotional disorders, may emotionally damage the participants much more than they benefit from being on the show.*

Other concerns focus more on the possible effects on a child's mental health and emotional development. Some worry that children will become so accustomed to all the attention that it will become difficult for them to adjust to normal life once the cameras stop following them around. These critics claim that losing this attention could cause the children to act out in negative ways. Also, the fact that children on reality shows are not playing a character but simply being themselves can make it more difficult and personal when people who watch the show say or post mean things on entertainment websites, social media sites, or blogs about the children.

Others are disturbed by the pressure on children featured in shows such as *Dance Moms* and *Toddlers and Tiaras*. They fear that the parents, eager for fame and fortune, sometimes ignore the needs of their children. Television critic Andy Denhart does not disagree with these criticisms, but he counters that good can come from these shows, too, and says, "There's certainly a

Do Clothing Makeover Shows Send the Wrong Message?

Personal makeover shows that target someone's wardrobe, rather than their actual body, are controversial in their own way. Take, for example, *What Not to Wear*, a show that airs on TLC in the United States and on the BBC in the United Kingdom. On this show, someone is selected whose clothing is considered unflattering, and stylists help that person discard items from their old wardrobe and make more flattering purchases in the future. Critics accuse these shows of encouraging people who are satisfied with the way they look to conform to others' ideas of what is fashionable.

Also, since most of the show's participants are nominated to be on the show by friends and/or coworkers, they can also be hurt to discover that the people they know find their wardrobe in need of replacement. Supporters point out that dressing more stylishly or age appropriately might help someone achieve greater success in business or personal relationships. They claim this is surely more important in the long run than a fondness for the beloved bowling shirts or oversized floral dresses that the participants are encouraged to discard.

lot of social value in illustrating the insane pressure adults place on kids while convincing themselves that it is for the kids' own good. TLC, Lifetime, and reality television producers did not create or cause this, and there's a possibility that broadcasting it could help stop it."[57]

Should People with Mental and Emotional Disorders Be on Reality Shows?

People have expressed doubt about the wisdom of inviting certain other groups of contestants besides children to participate on reality programs. Many also question whether the potential damage to participants in shows that focus on people with emotional disorders, such as *Hoarders*, outweighs the financial benefits to sponsors. Shows such as *Celebrity Rehab* and *Intervention* that feature participants with substance abuse problems have also been criticized. Programs like these have become very popular in the last few years, due to the public's fascination with dysfunctional lifestyles. As Julia Bricklin of *Forbes* magazine puts it, "We are . . . concerned with whether mom will finish off her bottle of mouthwash in order to maintain her alcoholic haze. . . . We want to know how grandma has managed to use diapers as her toilet for five years, and live with the stench, or how a trove of dogs and cats can die under a mountain of Campbell soup cans and uncle doesn't care."[58]

Hoarders and similar shows focus on people who hoard, or collect and hold on to items, to such a degree they are unable to care for either the items or themselves. The participants open doors and reveal rooms that are filled to the ceiling with belongings. Often on the show, the situation has become dangerous to the health of the people who live in the home. Garbage piles up in the kitchen; mice and roaches flee before the camera crews. Critics say these shows exploit people who hoard by exposing to public ridicule a very real, private struggle that impacts the hoarder's life and the lives of his or her family. While the shows offer immediate help by bringing in cleanup crews and psychologists, critics say this approach can be too much, too fast for a hoarder to handle. People sometimes become depressed after the camera crews leave and the interest in them disappears. Others, though, applaud the idea of exposing a problem that is often hidden. They feel that viewing the show might inspire other hoarders to recognize that they have a problem and seek help.

On A&E's *Intervention*, people with substance abuse problems are fooled into thinking they are being filmed for a documentary only to find themselves pressured by friends and family to check into a rehabilitation facility. Supporters of this program and similar ones believe that addicts viewing the show might be inspired to seek help. They also point out that the addicts featured on the shows are less likely to go back to their old ways because they can always view the footage and remind themselves about how unhealthy they were and how much progress they have made. And many of those who appear on these programs are indeed helped: A&E posts follow-up videos on its website that look in on success stories after episodes have aired, and several of those who appeared on *Celebrity Rehab* have credited the show with changing their lives for the better.

Some people, however, question whether the addicts are actually legally competent to sign the paperwork to participate on the show. Some people may not realize, for one thing, that a permanent—and potentially damaging—video record will now exist that shows them at the lowest point in their lives. As Matthew Gilbert of the *Boston Globe* puts it, "Does anyone truly think that people lost in addiction are clear-thinking enough to choose whether to put their stories on TV for public consumption? Is an addict hitting his bottom in the position to sign away images of himself hitting his bottom?"[59] Recovering addicts have also claimed that the show makes the process of getting clean look much easier than it actually is.

Dangers to Cast Members

Sometimes production crews on shows devoted to substance abuse have been accused of endangering participants in their eagerness for footage. Former teen star Leif Garrett, who appeared on VH1's *Celebrity Rehab*, claimed that the show's producers talked him into using drugs so they could film his drug use for the show, even though he had been clean for four days in the hopes of getting a head start on his rehab. (VH1 denies this.) On one episode of *Intervention*, the on-site producer allowed an addict on the show to drive off in a car, despite the fact she was clearly very drunk. While this might seem wrong or unethical, it is not illegal. As lawyer Michael J. O'Connor explains, "Television producers are not policemen. On a moral level, you get to the point where stepping in seems like it would be something you'd want to do. But from a legal standpoint, third parties causing injuries to other third parties is not something a television program is really responsible for."[60] The show's creator and executive producer, Sam Mettler, claims that on many other occasions he personally stopped someone from driving while intoxicated and once talked down a drug addict who threatened to commit suicide.

Physical danger to participants is not unique to substance abuse shows, and sometimes the danger comes not from the production crew, but from fellow cast members. On several occasions, cast members have participated on reality shows despite having been in trouble with the law for physical altercations, an indication that they have quick tempers and might potentially put their fellow cast members at risk. On VH1's *Megan Wants a Millionaire*, one of the contestants, Ryan Jenkins, had a police record for assaulting an ex-girlfriend, something that the show's background check failed to reveal. (After the show began airing, Jenkins killed his wife, ran from police, and ended up committing suicide in a hotel room.) On the second season of *Big Brother*, Justin Sebik held a knife to the throat of another Houseguest. It was later discovered that Sebik had been arrested three times for assault, but the charges had been dismissed. In 2003 police raided the house used by *The Real World: San Diego* while the show was filming to investigate a report that a woman was raped in the bathroom by a friend of one of the participants. In early 2012 Alex Da Silva, one of the choreographers on *So You Think You Can Dance*, was sentenced to ten years in prison for a rape he had committed in 2002 and an attempted rape in 2009. Another choreographer on the show, Shane Sparks, who also served as a judge on *America's Best Dance Crew*, pled no contest in 2011 to charges of having had sex with a minor under sixteen. Sparks served 270 days in jail.

So You Think You Can Dance choreographer Shane Sparks pled no contest to child molestation charges in 2011 and served 270 days in jail.

Of course, people with criminal backgrounds also work on scripted shows. However, participants on reality shows usually work with fewer legal protections, since the contracts they sign state outright that the producers are not responsible for bad things that may happen during filming. It can be especially risky to have participants with violent tendencies and short fuses on programs in which the producers are actively working to create conflict between cast members to make the show more exciting.

Reality Television's Effect on Young Viewers

So what does all this mean for young viewers of reality television? Are these programs—and all the debates and scandals surrounding them—hurtful to children and teens? Or are reality shows just harmless entertainment? As with most aspects of the genre, opinions are mixed.

Some sources believe that much of reality programming is a bad influence on today's youth. The Parents Television Council (PTC), for example, voices many concerns about the effects of reality programs on children, and it has completed several studies on the genre. In one, the council counted and analyzed the number of sexual references, curse words, and incidents of violence that occurred in twenty-nine different reality shows from June 2002 to August 2003. The study found that there were 9.9 instances of foul language per hour in the reality shows that were reviewed, 4.3 sexual references, and 0.26 instances of violence. (It should be noted that the violent acts the study measured did not include the relational aggression mentioned earlier.) The PTC concluded: "Reality television is now a fixture on programming schedules and parents need to be aware that although these series are promoted heavily and often tailor-made for young viewers, they are almost never appropriate for impressionable young minds."[61]

A 2011 study by the PTC focused on four of the most popular reality programs on MTV (*Jersey Shore*, *Teen Mom*, *16 and Pregnant*, and *The Real World*) and how they portrayed the behavior of men and women. The council was concerned that these shows were influencing the social development of young girls and boys. The study found that only 24 percent of what women on these shows said about themselves was positive and that women said more bad things than men when talking about themselves or other women. It also found that of the many references to sex made on the programs, only 4 percent of them involved virginity, contraception, or sexually transmitted diseases. The PTC concluded, "There remains an overwhelming message to young girls that their only unique and valued quality is their sexuality. The message to males is that they should lack [outward] emotion, be uninterested in relationships, and be defined by sexual conquests."[62]

However, even the PTC admits that some educational reality shows are worthwhile. And others believe that reality show critics underestimate today's youth and their ability to tell fact from fiction and right from wrong. Louisa Stein, head of Critical Studies in Television, Film, and New Media at San Diego State University, says that she believes young people today often watch reality programs to criticize them and make fun of them, rather than to imitate the behavior on them. As journalist Margaret Bernstein states, "Raised on a steady diet of reality TV, YouTube, and Facebook, young people today are exceptionally media literate, and are quite used to observing, rating and [criticizing] the personal stories they see spilling across their television screens."[63]

In addition, other studies report some positive aspects of reality television. The Girl Scouts poll found that 75 percent of those who responded said that reality shows inspired conversation with their parents and/or friends. Sixty-eight percent said that reality programs made them feel like they could achieve anything, and 48 percent said the shows made them realize there were other people in the world like themselves. Sixty-two percent reported that reality shows had raised their awareness of social causes and issues, and 59 percent said they had learned new things from watching reality television.

Experts agree that parents should monitor the shows their children are viewing and should watch their children's favorite reality programs with them. Then the parents can discuss with the children what they are seeing and help them sort through the messages—both positive and negative—that the shows deliver. Many media scholars believe that with strong guidance from adults, children can learn to watch reality television in an educated, critical manner and not be affected by the bad behavior shown on some programs.

THE INFLUENCE AND FUTURE OF REALITY TELEVISION

When it first became widespread in the early 2000s, reality programming was considered by some to be a passing fad that would not last very long. Over a decade later, however, the genre is still going strong; it even has its own categories at the Emmy Awards. College courses on reality television are now offered at schools such as Indiana University and San Jose State University. An essay question on reality television appeared on the Scholastic Aptitude Test, or SAT, in 2011. (This led some people to protest that the question was not fair to those who do not watch such programming.) Many forms of media reference reality programming on an increasingly common basis, even in articles that have nothing to do with television. For example, in an article about the presidential debate between Barack Obama and Mitt Romney held on October 3, 2012, columnist Gail Collins mused on whether or not undecided viewers had tuned into the debate by saying, "Maybe they [did], under the impression that it's another reality show about pawnbrokers, except this time they wear really nice suits."[64] Even disasters can't drive reality television from the public's mind. After Hurricane Sandy ravaged the shore of New Jersey in October 2012, Governor Chris Christie stated in an interview that aired on NY1 News, "I've never seen devastation like this in my life. Not here in New Jersey. You know, you see sites like the Seaside Heights boardwalk, where the program the *Jersey Shore* is filmed . . . the boardwalk is gone. It is gone."[65] The NY1 anchors also commented that the

Jersey Shore cast members were tweeting about the hurricane. Reality television is more than firmly fastened to today's popular culture. It has become a reality of everyday life.

Reality's Influence

Reality shows have had a notable influence on other forms of entertainment. The genre's influence on its scripted television counterpart is often obvious. Scripted programs such as *The Office*, *Modern Family*, and *Parks and Recreation* are filmed documentary style and make use of "confessional" interviews with characters who speak directly to the camera. These are not unlike interviews one sees with participants in reality shows such as *The Bachelor*, *Survivor*, and *The Real World*. In 2011 and 2012 ABC's supernatural thriller *The River* was presented entirely as if it were footage from a documentary being filmed. ABC's crime drama *Detroit 1-8-7* was also originally intended to be shot documentary style, as if a camera crew were following around the homicide detective characters. However, the deadly 2010 incident involving the reality police show *The First 48*, also filmed in Detroit, resulted in the production team changing the setup of the program to a more standard format.

Other scripted television shows have been developed in an attempt to cash in on the popularity of a particular reality program. Sources report that the hugely successful *Lost* came about because ABC asked show creator J.J. Abrams to come up with a scripted version of *Survivor*. And *Glee*, which features pop songs sung by its characters, owes much to the appeal of *American Idol*. (*Glee* has in turn spawned its own reality program, *The Glee Project*, in which contestants compete for a chance to appear on the scripted show.)

As for the big screen, the documentary-film style is evident there, too. One of the most well-known examples is *The Blair Witch Project*, which was released in 1999. The film follows three students who travel into the woods of Burkittsville, Maryland, to film a documentary about a local legend, the Blair Witch. The students disappear in the woods, and *The Blair Witch Project* is supposedly the footage filmed by the three students that was recovered after they disappeared. Although this technique has

Reality shows have had a notable influence on other forms of entertainment. The 1999 movie The Blair Witch Project *(the cast of which is shown here) used documentary-film techniques influenced by the reality show semidocumentary format.*

become more common, it was unique at the time, and many people believed that the film documented real events. Other, more recent, movies filmed in this style include *Cloverfield*, *Project X*, and the *Paranormal Activity* series.

In addition, moviegoers have become more familiar with the concept of mixing reality and storytelling, which has resulted in an increase in films based on true stories. As Steven Zeitchik wrote in the *Los Angeles Times*, "Experts say that after a decade of reality television, the film business is finally catching up. Audiences and studio executives now not only tolerate a dose of real life in their feature films, they expect it. Stories . . . go from ordinary to powerful in the minds of filmgoers the moment 'based on a true story' flashes across the screen."[66] Some examples of such films in the last few years include *127 Hours*, *The Social Network*, *We Bought a Zoo*, and *Moneyball*.

Even the world of publishing has been affected by reality television, with concepts from reality programming appearing in the storylines of books. Perhaps the best-known example of this is the wildly popular trilogy *The Hunger Games*. These futuristic books center on a fight-to-the-death competition between children that is televised live to citizens.

Reality TV and the Internet

The Internet and reality programming also enjoy a mutually beneficial relationship. The Internet and reality television have been closely linked for a long time. The Internet has served as an influence, companion, and additional source of reality programming. The "fly-on-the-wall" concept of watching things happen in real time has been present on the World Wide Web for many years. The first live image to be shown on the Internet via webcam was that of a coffeepot in the Trojan Room at England's Cambridge University. A team of scientists set up the webcam in 1993 to check whether or not there was any coffee in the pot before they left their offices and headed down several flights of stairs to the Trojan Room. The site was live until 2001, by which time it had attracted 2.4 million visitors, despite showing nothing more thrilling than the coffeepot slowly filling and being emptied. According to Dan Gordon, one of the scientists, "Once, some American tourists called into the tourist information center here and asked where [the coffeepot] was so they could visit it. . . . They took lots of photos."[67]

It was not long before webcam broadcasts began to feature human subjects. One of the first and most well known was Jennifer Ringley, creator of JenniCam. Ringley set up a webcam in her college dorm room in 1996 and broadcast images that refreshed every three minutes. After relocating to Washington, D.C., in 1998, Ringley set up more cameras and began charging a fee through PayPal for users to see more-frequent uploads. Ringley's cameras revealed every activity, from commonplace tasks such as brushing her hair or playing with her pets to more intimate activities such as bringing dates back to her apartment. According to CNN.com, Ringley said in her mission statement, "I keep JenniCam alive not because I want or need to be watched, but because I simply don't mind being watched."[68] At its most popular, the site received 4 million hits per day. Ringley shut down JenniCam at the end of 2003 after PayPal canceled her account due to objections over the broadcasting of some of her

YouTube and Reality Television

YouTube is a popular website that allows people to upload videos and share them with the public. In effect, this provides an outlet for anyone to create his or her own reality show and post it for others to see. People can also showcase their talents by uploading a YouTube video of themselves singing or dancing, which is much easier than auditioning for a talent competition such as *American Idol* or *So You Think You Can Dance*. Several popular singers, such as Justin Bieber and Charice, first gained popularity on YouTube.

YouTube also serves as an outlet for people who are already known in the entertainment business. In 2010 Kelly Cutrone of Bravo's *Kell on Earth* created her own YouTube channel so she could continue to communicate with fans after her show had finished filming. Also in 2010, hearing-impaired actress Marlee Matlin produced a reality series on YouTube called *My Deaf Family*, which was about a California family with several deaf members. She turned to YouTube after trying to sell the show to various networks that were reluctant to handle a show with subtitles and sign language.

The YouTube website allows people to post their own versions of reality programming.

more private moments. However, many other web broadcasters followed in her footsteps, helping feed the public's desire for live entertainment both on the web and on television. Webcam broadcasts today allow viewers to monitor such diverse sights as the nest of a pair of red-tailed hawks in New York's Washington Square Park, the panda enclosure at the San Diego Zoo, and the numbers of cars waiting to get a ferry from Anacortes to the San Juan Islands in Washington State.

In other cases the Internet and reality television shows have operated as broadcast partners. One of the better-known partnerships is the live twenty-four-hour webcam feeds that accompany seasons of CBS's *Big Brother*. Although only some of the footage captured by the cameras set up throughout the *Big Brother* compound is shown on the television episodes, viewers can log on to the Internet feed from the house at any time of day or night and see unedited footage of the inhabitants. Another example of the Internet working with a reality show is NBC's *Fashion Star*, a *Project Runway*–like program, which allows viewers to go online the day after an episode airs and buy the clothes created by the contestants. Viewers of *American Idol* and *The Voice* are able to cast votes for their favorite contestant by downloading that contestant's song from iTunes.

A WINDOW TO OTHER CULTURES

"Reality TV can be educational and realistic. Shows like *The Amazing Race* widen viewers' knowledge about travel and different cultures around the globe, presenting amazing landscapes and history in a fun and addictive way people can learn from."
—New Zealander Meghan Pilkington, age twelve.

Meghan Pilkington. "A Dose of Reality Can Be Good—in Moderation." *New Zealand Herald*, September 20, 2011. www.nzherald.co.nz/college-herald/news/article.cfm?c_id=1502920&objectid=10753863.

Some reality shows are broadcast entirely on the Internet. For example, *Our Prisoner*, which aired online in 2006 and was streamed live twenty-four hours a day, featured a thirty-five-year-old man named Kieran Vogel. Viewers of the program voted to control all Vogel's actions—what he wore, what he ate, who he dated, and so on. Also in 2006, NBC broadcast *Star Tomorrow*, a musical talent search similar to *American Idol*, on the Internet. *The Next Internet Millionaire* completed a season online in 2007. The show was similar to *The Apprentice* in that contestants were asked to finish a series of tasks related to Internet marketing. Similar to *Our Prisoner*, in 2010 *Control TV* featured a continuous, live stream of an ordinary man named Tristan Couvares. The show's viewers voted to control certain aspects of Couvares's life, such as his haircut and choice of pet. The show's producers claimed the program received 50,000 votes per day, with one episode hitting 170,000 votes.

In 2011 the website YouNow was launched, with its creators claiming that it was the "web's first online reality network."[69]

The founder of YouNow, Adi Sideman (standing), speaks about YouNow's website, which, he claims, is the "web's first online reality network."

The site is a social entertainment platform where users upload live video of themselves and receive feedback on the content from the website's audience in real time. The audience votes on whether or not to award the person in the video more online air time. The creators refer to the site as a "modern-day *Gong Show*,"[70] referring to a talent-based game show from the 1970s and 1980s in which people performed in front of judges who either let them finish (if the performance was good) or struck a giant gong to stop the act if it was bad. Another site, YouToo, lets users upload fifteen-second video files called "Fame Spots" that are then aired on the company's television channel.

Reality TV and Social Media

Social media outlets such as Facebook, Twitter, and posting boards on websites also link together reality television and the Internet. Producer Mark Burnett credits the success of some shows to social media. He refers to social media as the "electronic water cooler"[71] and claims that the Internet is where people now go to discuss a show rather than gathering around the water cooler at work. And viewers do not even have to wait until a show is over to discuss it—Twitter and applications such as Into Now and Get Glue allow people to comment on a program in real time while it is airing. In fact, shows such as *Dancing with the Stars* and *The Voice* have taken to publishing on-screen some of the tweets sent in by fans during the show. In 2012 the *Hollywood Reporter* conducted a poll on social media and the impact of Facebook and Twitter on entertainment users. The poll revealed the strong effect of social media on television: Three out of ten people responded that they watched a television show because of something they saw on a social media site. Seventy-six percent of those polled said they posted about shows while watching them live, and 41 percent reported tweeting about the show they were watching. Forty-six percent of respondents claimed that reality programs were the ones about which they were most likely to post comments.

Some reality competitions allow viewers to cast votes through social media outlets. *The X Factor* offers fans the option to vote through Twitter, and *The Voice* and *Idol* let viewers cast votes through Facebook. These voting methods concern some fans, however. One poster on the Television Without Pity forums responded to the news about *The Voice*'s Facebook application by saying, "In terms of using social media to vote, I'd find it much sketchier if [*The Voice*] allowed voting through Twitter (through use of a hash tag or something along those lines). . . . I fear the power voting could get out of control if someone with a ton of followers like [Justin] Bieber or Kim Kardashian started urging their fans to retweet a hash-tagged vote for one contestant."[72] This comment was posted partly in response to an incident during *The Voice*'s first season, when Justin Bieber encouraged his Twitter followers to vote for Javier Colon. Colon won the competition, and some claimed the victory was an outcome of Bieber's influence rather than Colon's personal popularity.

SOME SHOWS DO NOT EDUCATE

"[Shows like *Real Housewives* and *Keeping Up with the Kardashians*] are not about [the] quiet grace and dignity of everyday living. It's about a bunch of people who don't have any ambition beyond going out to lunch and owning things. There's nothing really to, you know, challenge your brain."—TV critic Mary McNamara.

Quoted in Jeff Greenfield. "The Real Deal on Reality TV." CBSNews.com, September 5, 2010. www.cbsnews.com/2100-3445_162-6183037.html.

Facebook fan pages and posting forums such as those on Television Without Pity have become very popular with viewers, and producers pay attention to this. They sometimes assign staff members to read the posts and Twitter feeds and see what the fans are saying. Producers also sometimes work with cast members to create Facebook profiles that provide viewers with more personal information about the cast members. Indeed, some shows require stars to maintain and update personal social media accounts. The producers of *American Idol* even managed to find a way to profit from Facebook. In 2011 they offered users the chance to send video messages from the contestants to other Facebook users for one dollar. As the popularity of social media continues to rise, reality show creators will likely continue to seek new ways to connect reality television and social media. Simon Cowell once dismissed the effect of Twitter on his shows but has acknowledged his error and even stated, "The only powerful people now on TV are the people on Twitter and Facebook."[73]

The Future of Reality Television

With the growing influence of social media, it seems likely that reality television will continue well into the foreseeable future. According to Herb Terry, who developed the course on reality television at Indiana University, "We've been saying for years that the future of television would no longer be as a stand-alone medium, that it would be a medium that would somehow interact with everything else. Reality TV may be the best example running right now."[74] Indeed, because many of its programs depend on audience interaction, reality television seems far ahead of scripted programming in this respect.

The cost factor is another reason that reality programming will likely survive indefinitely; it is much cheaper to produce a reality show than it is to produce a scripted one. Sources in the entertainment business claim that it costs around $700,000 to $1.6 million to produce an hour of reality television, while it costs $2 million to $3 million to produce an hour of scripted programming. One reason for this cost savings is that reality show cast members earn less than actors on scripted programs. Producers also save money because the writers on reality shows are not covered by Writers Guild of America (WGA) contracts. As a result, the writers have no guaranteed wages or standard benefits such as health insurance. (This has been a major source of debate in the television industry, because the WGA believes this is not fair to the writers.)

It is hard to predict exactly how reality programming will unfold in the near future, but the genre appears to be continuing to explore a wide variety of topics and issues. A glance at a recent list of casting calls reveals that reality producers are looking for grandmothers and grandfathers who cook, stay-at-home dads, Valley girls, bargain hunters, children of celebrities, licensed therapists, real estate agents, and moms of cheerleaders. Reality producers seem willing to try to make almost any subject interesting to the viewing public—for a profit.

What Some People Will Do to Get a Reality Show

Many people dream of being the star of their own reality program. For most, dreaming is as far as it goes. But some hopefuls have gone to great—and illegal—lengths to attract attention.

In 2009 Richard and Mayumi Heene (who had formerly appeared twice on *Wife Swap*) contacted police, tearfully claiming that a large helium balloon had taken off with their six-year-old son inside. A massive rescue effort was launched, and it seemed the entire world was watching in horror as the balloon drifted across the Colorado skies. When the balloon finally landed, however, the boy was not inside. He was later found hiding in the attic of his home. It turned out that the entire inci-dent was a stunt concocted by the Heenes to generate publicity in hopes of landing their own reality show. The Heenes were fined and served jail time for the stunt.

Also in 2009, Tareq and Michaele Salahi showed up uninvited to a dinner at the White House. The two were being considered as cast members for Bravo's show *The Real Housewives of D.C.* at the time and were filmed by a crew while preparing for the evening. When it was revealed that they were not actually on the guest list, the Salahis were investigated by a federal grand jury. In spite of the federal investigation, they managed to reach their goal and became part of the *Housewives* cast.

Tareq and Michaele Salahi testify at a hearing regarding their crashing of a White House state dinner as a publicity stunt. The couple later became cast members on The Real Housewives of D.C.

At least one producer believes that expanding the target audience may be the key to expanding the genre's reach. Gil Goldschein, the president of Bunim/Murray Productions, says that his company has become interested in producing shows aimed at seven- to fourteen-year-olds. He also says Bunim/Murray is looking into opportunities to partner with on-demand media streaming platforms such as Netflix and Hulu. Others in the entertainment business believe the future will bring new twists and tweaks to the formats of reality programs currently on the air. In a 2012 interview with the *Hollywood Reporter*, producer Jonathan Murray reflected on how reality television has had to evolve over the years. When asked if he thought *The Real World* would sell at MTV if he pitched it to them today, he said, "I'm not sure we could sell it today. It's almost too pure, and it doesn't have a lot of bells and whistles. Today you start with a *Real World* idea of either putting people in a house, then you have to add the additional elements— they're all bad girls, they're all from the Jersey Shore—to make it loud enough to capture people's attention."[75]

One thing is certain: Debates over the value of reality television will continue as long as it continues to exert a powerful force in the entertainment business. As long as the popularity of reality programming continues and profits grow, critics of reality television seem to fight a losing battle. Does reality television grant fame and fortune to people who do not seem to deserve it? In some cases. Does it showcase bad behavior? Occasionally. Do cast members look and act ridiculous? Sometimes. But reality television also amuses, comforts, and educates. According to television critic James Poniewozik:

> There are . . . American ideas that reality TV taps into: That everybody should have a shot. That sometimes being real is better than being polite. That no matter where you started out, you can hit it big, get lucky and reinvent yourself. . . . And most important, that you can find something interesting in the lives of people other than celebrities, lawyers and doctors. . . . It is as if, as a society, we had been singing in front of a mirror for generations, only to discover that now the mirror can actually see us. And if we are really lucky, it might just offer us a show.[76]

Introduction: A Power in Television Today

1. Neil Genzlinger. "Have I Got a Show for You. . . ." *New York Times*, March 31, 2011. www.nytimes.com/2011/04/03/arts /television/reality-shows-can-you-guess-the-fakes.html ?pagewanted=all.
2. James Poniewozik. "Why Reality TV Is Good for Us." *Time*, February 12, 2003. www.time.com/time/magazine/article /0,9171,421047,00.html.
3. Quoted in Michael Ventre. "Will 2011 Be the Year Reality TV Dies?" *Today*, January 3, 2011. http://today.msnbc.msn .com/id/40753472/ns/today-entertainment/t/will-be-year -reality-tv-dies.

Chapter 1: What Is Reality Television?

4. Quoted in David S. Escoffery, ed. *How Real Is Reality TV?* Jefferson, NC: McFarland, 2006, pp. 29–30.
5. Robin Nabi, Erica Biely, Sara Morgan, and Carmen Stitt. "Reality-Based Television Programming and the Psychology of Its Appeal." *Media Psychology*, December 2003, p. 304.
6. Matthew Gilbert. "The House That Roared." *Boston Globe*, March 6, 2011. www.boston.com/ae/tv/articles/2011/03/06 /mtvs_the_real_world_has_influenced_a_generation_of _reality_shows/?page=1.
7. Andy Denhart. "25 Seasons On, *Real World* as Immature as Ever." *Today*, March 14, 2011. http://today.msnbc.msn .com/id/41987240/ns/today-entertainment.
8. Mark Andrejevic. *Reality TV: The Work of Being Watched.* Lanham, MD: Rowman & Littlefield, 2004, p. 72.
9. Quoted in Edward Wong. "China TV Grows Racy, and Gets a Chaperon." *New York Times*, December 31, 2011. www

.nytimes.com/2012/01/01/world/asia/censors-pull-reins-as
-china-tv-chasing-profit-gets-racy.html?pagewanted=1.

10. Quoted in Sarah Anne Hughes. "China's *Super Girl* Talent Show Canceled for Being Too Democratic?" *Washington Post*, September 19, 2011. www.washingtonpost.com/blogs /blogpost/post/chinas-super-girl-talent-show-canceled-for -being-too-democratic/2011/09/19/gIQAYthsfK_blog.html.

11. Quoted in Ashley Fantz. "Reality Shows Revolutionize Arab TV." CNN.com, March 17, 2012. http://www.cnn.com/2012 /03/17/world/arab-reality-shows/index.html?hpt=hp_bn7.

12. Naomi Sakr. *Arab Media and Political Renewal*. New York: Tauris, 2007, p. 49.

13. Yvonne Villarreal. "'Real World' Keeps Turning, and Keeps Viewers Tuning In." *Los Angeles Times*, March 9, 2011. http://articles.latimes.com/2011/mar/09/entertainment/la -et-real-world-20110309.

Chapter 2: Why Do People Watch Reality Television?

14. Eric Jaffe. "Reality Check." *Observer*, March 2005. www .psychologicalscience.org/observer/getArticle.cfm?id=1742.

15. Quoted in Jaffe. "Reality Check."

16. Escoffery. *How Real Is Reality TV?*, p. 107.

17. Christopher Bell. *American Idolatry: Celebrity, Commodity, and Reality Television*. Jefferson, NC: McFarland, 2010, p. 75.

18. Quoted in Jesse Hicks. "Why Do We Love Reality Television?" ResearchPennState, August 24, 2009. www.rps.psu .edu/probing/realitytv.html.

19. Sandra Gonzalez. "Dance Moms: Why Am I So Fascinated?" *PopWatch* (blog), *Entertainment Weekly*, January 25, 2012. http://popwatch.ew.com/2012/01/25/dance-moms.

20. Sydney Lipez. Personal interview with the author, March 2012.

21. Quoted in Escoffery. *How Real Is Reality TV?*, p. 71.

22. Poniewozik. "Why Reality TV Is Good for Us."

23. Andy Denhart. "'Here Comes Honey Boo Boo' Blows Up." *Daily Beast*, September 12, 2012. www.thedailybeast.com

/articles/2012/09/12/here-comes-honey-boo-boo-blows-up
.html.

24. Quoted in Jeff Grabmeier. "New Theory of Motivation
Lists 16 Basic Desires That Guide Us." *Ohio State Research
News*, June 28, 2000. http://researchnews.osu.edu/archive
/whoami.htm.

25. Steven Reiss and James Wiltz. "Why America Loves Reality
TV." *Psychology Today*, September 1, 2001. www.psychology
today.com/articles/200109/why-america-loves-reality-tv.

26. Steven Reiss and James Wiltz. "Why People Watch Reality
TV." *Media Psychology*, 2004, pp. 373–374.

27. Robin Nabi, Carmen R. Stitt, Jeff Halford, and Keli L. Finnerty. "Emotional and Cognitive Predictors of the Enjoyment
of Reality-Based and Fictional Television Programming: An
Elaboration of the Uses and Gratifications Perspective." *Media Psychology*, 2006, pp. 431–432.

Chapter 3: The "Reality" of Reality Television

28. Joanne Ostrow. "How Real Are Reality Shows?" *Pittsburgh
Post-Gazette*, March 20, 2010. http://old.post-gazette.com
/pg/10079/1044191-67.stm?cmpid=entertainment.xml.

29. Quoted in Keith Hollihan. "The Omarosa Experiment."
Morning News, January 17, 2006. www.themorningnews
.org/article/the-omarosa-experiment.

30. Quoted in Bell. *American Idolatry*, p. 43.

31. Quoted in Camille Dodero. "We Have Obtained a Copy of
MTV's Standard *Real World* Cast-Member Contract." *Village
Voice*, August 1, 2011. http://blogs.villagevoice.com/runnin
scared/2011/08/mtv_real_world_contract.php?page=2.

32. Quoted in Jeff Greenfield. "The Real Deal on Reality TV."
CBS News, September 5, 2010. www.cbsnews.com/2100
-3445_162-6183037.html.

33. Quoted in Richard Huff. *Reality Television*. Westport, CT:
Praeger, 2006, p. 172.

34. Derek Woodruff. Personal communication with author,
March 2012.

35. Quoted in Andrejevic. *Reality TV*, p. 104.

36. Quoted in Hollihan. "The Omarosa Experiment."

37. Quoted in Hollihan. "The Omarosa Experiment."

38. Quoted in Craig Thomashoff. "Casting Reality TV? It's Now Difficult to Find Real People." *New York Times*, August 25, 2011. www.nytimes.com/2011/08/28/arts/television/casting -reality-tv-has-become-more-difficult.html.

39. Edward Wyatt. "TV Contestants: Tired, Tipsy, and Pushed to the Brink." *New York Times*, August 2, 2009. www.ny times.com/2009/08/02/business/media/02reality.html ?pagewanted=all.

40. Quoted in Carrie Brownstein. "*The Bachelor* and Other De-lights," *Monitor Mix* (blog), NPR.org, April 28, 2008. www .npr.org/blogs/monitormix/2008/04/the_bachelor_1.html.

41. Quoted in Kim Reed. "It's Time to Stop Blaming the Edit-ing." *Today*, November 29, 2004. http://today.msnbc.msn .com/id/6407884/ns/today-entertainment/t/its-time-stop -blaming-editing.

42. Fox.com. "So You Think You Can Dance Season 8 Voting Frequently Asked Questions." June 9, 2011. http://dance .blogs.fox.com/2011/06/09/so-you-think-you-can-dance -season-8-voting-frequently-asked-questions.

43. Quoted in Joal Ryan. "No 'Idol' Controversy." *E! Online*, August 20, 2002. www.eonline.com/news/No__quot_Idol _quot__Controversy/43755.

44. Quoted in Lyndsey Parker. "Ex-*Idol* Contestant Says Show Is Rigged." Yahoo! Music, July 29, 2009. http://music.yahoo .com/blogs/reality-rocks/ex-idol-contestant-says-show-is -rigged.html.

45. Quoted in Monica Rizzo. "*Dancing* Producer Responds to Voting Controversy." *People*, November 19, 2010. www .people.com/people/article/0,,20443659,00.html.

46. Quoted in Scott Collins. "*Idol*'s AT&T Voting Flap Is Con-troversy as Usual at Fox." *Los Angeles Times*, May 28, 2009. http://articles.latimes.com/2009/may/28/entertainment/et -american-idol28.

Chapter 4: Is Reality Television Harmful to Society?

47. James Poniewozik, "Television: Why Reality TV Is Good for Us." *Time*, February 17, 2003. www.time.com/time/magazine/article/0,9171,1004251-1,00.html.

48. Quoted in Andrea Canning and Elizabeth Stuart. "Reality Show Violence Getting Too Real?" ABC News, March 30, 2011. http://abcnews.go.com/Entertainment/reality-tv-show-violence-real-life-consequences-teen/story?id=13256971.

49. Quoted in Hollie McKay. "Reality Shows Aimed at Young Viewers Airing More Violent Scenes." Fox News, October 11, 2010. www.foxnews.com/entertainment/2010/10/11/reality-shows-battery-domestic-violence-jersey-shore-teen-mom.

50. Quoted in Liane Bonin Starr. "Do You Have to Be Crazy to Be a Reality TV Star?" *Starr Raving* (blog), Hit Fix, September 1, 2011. www.hitfix.com/blogs/starr-raving/posts/do-you-have-to-be-crazy-to-be-a-reality-tv-star.

51. Quoted in Brendan Borrell. "Pros, Cons of Reality TV's Approach to Weight Loss." *Los Angeles Times*, January 31, 2011. http://articles.latimes.com/2011/jan/31/health/la-he-weight-loss-reality-shows-20110131.

52. Jennifer L. Pozner. *Reality Bites Back: The Troubling Truth About Guilty Pleasure TV*. Berkeley, CA: Seal, 2010, p. 54.

53. Quoted in CBS. *The Amazing Race*. February 26, 2012.

54. Quoted in CBS. *The Amazing Race*. March 25, 2012.

55. Allison Samuels. "Reality TV Trashes Black Women." *Daily Beast*, May 1, 2011. www.thedailybeast.com/newsweek/2011/05/01/reality-tv-trashes-black-women.html.

56. Quoted in Greg Braxton. "*The Bachelor, The Bachelorette* Creator Defends All-White Cast of Title Role." *Los Angeles Times*, March 18, 2011. http://articles.latimes.com/2011/mar/18/entertainment/la-et-bachelor-race-20110318.

57. Andy Denhart. "*Dance Moms, Toddlers & Tiaras*, and Child Abuse." *Daily Beast*, January 25, 2012. www.thedailybeast.com/articles/2012/01/25/dance-moms-toddlers-tiaras-and-child-abuse.html.

58. Julia Bricklin. "Monday Night Rehab: A&E's *Intervention* and *Hoarders* Return." *Forbes*, January 3, 2012. www.forbes

.com/sites/juliabricklin/2012/01/03/monday-night-rehab
-aes-intervention-and-hoarders-return.

59. Matthew Gilbert. "Hooked." *Boston Globe*, March 14, 2010.
www.boston.com/ae/tv/articles/2010/03/14/do_reality
_shows_merely_exploit_addicts__or_give_them_a_shot_at
_redemption/?page=2.

60. Quoted in Jeremy W. Peters. "When Reality TV Gets Too
Real." *New York Times*, October 8, 2007. www.nytimes.com
/2007/10/08/business/media/08reality.html?pagewanted
=all.

61. Aubree Rankin. "Reality TV: Race to the Bottom." Parents
Television Council. www.parentstv.org/PTC/publications
/reports/realitytv2/main.asp.

62. Parents Television Council. "Reality on MTV: Gender Por-
trayals on MTV Reality Programming." 2011. www.parent
stv.org/PTC/publications/reports/MTV-RealityStudy/MTV
RealityStudy_Dec11.pdf.

63. Margaret Bernstein. "Does Reality TV for Teens Induce Bad
Behavior?" Cleveland.com, March 15, 2008. www.cleveland
.com/entertainment/index.ssf/2008/03/does_reality_tv_for
_teens_indu.html.

Chapter 5: The Influence and
Future of Reality Television

64. Gail Collins. "Bobbing Along on a Sea of Debate Coverage,"
Salt Lake (UT) Tribune, October 4, 2012. www.sltrib.com
/sltrib/opinion/55025308-82/debate-mitt-season-barack
.html.csp.

65. Chris Christie. NY1 News, October 31, 2012.

66. Steven Zeitchik. "From Real to Reel: In Fact-Based Films,
Reality and Storytelling Collide." *Los Angeles Times*, December 27, 2010. http://articles.latimes.com/2010/dec/27/enter
tainment/la-et-movie-reality-20101227.

67. Quoted in *Wired*. "Farewell, Seminal Coffee Cam." March 7,
2001. www.wired.com/culture/lifestyle/news/2001/03/42254.

68. Quoted in CNN.com. "Voyeur Web Site JenniCam to Go Dark." December 10, 2003. www.cnn.com/2003/TECH/internet/12/10/jenni.cam.reut.

69. YouNow. "Terms of Use." www.younow.com.

70. YouNow. "Terms of Use."

71. Quoted in Michael Stelzner. "Social Media and Reality TV: How Mark Burnett Is Leading the Way." November 11, 2010. www.socialmediaexaminer.com/social-media-and-reality-tv-how-mark-burnett-is-leading-the-way/.

72. KerleyQ. TelevisionWithoutPity.com, March 31, 2012. http://forums.televisionwithoutpity.com/index.php?showtopic=3203407&st=4860.

73. Quoted in Brian Stelter. "Twitter and TV Get Close to Help Each Other Grow." *New York Times*, October 25, 2011. www.nytimes.com/2011/10/26/business/media/twitter-and-tv-get-close-to-help-each-other-grow.html.

74. Quoted in IU News Room. "Reality Television Not Just Fun Viewing for IU Students, but Also a Serious College Course." News release, October 13, 2003. http://newsinfo.iu.edu/news/page/normal/1148.html.

75. Quoted in Lacey Rose and Stacey Wilson. "Bunim/Murray at 25." *Hollywood Reporter*, April 6, 2012, p. 55.

76. James Poniewozik. "Reality TV at 10: How It's Changed Television—and Us." *Time*, February 22, 2010. www.time.com/time/magazine/article/0,9171,1963739-4,00.html.

DISCUSSION QUESTIONS

Chapter 1: What Is Reality Television?

1. According to the author, why is reality television difficult to define?

2. Why is it so hard to divide reality shows into categories? Which shows besides those mentioned by the author do not seem to fit neatly into any of the categories listed in chapter one?

3. In what ways do reality television shows in Asia and the Middle East differ from those in the United States?

Chapter 2: Why Do People Watch Reality Television?

1. The author says that one reason people watch reality television is that they like to watch ordinary people like themselves. Why do you think this is?

2. Why do you think people enjoy watching celebrities do the same things and deal with the same problems as ordinary people?

3. Steven Reiss's study concluded that people who like the idea of vengeance (getting revenge) enjoy reality programs. How do these programs satisfy this desire?

Chapter 3: The "Reality" of Reality Television

1. Aside from "bad boy" and "party girl," what are some other typical characters (stereotypes) frequently depicted on reality programs?

2. Many reality show contracts give the producers the right to do whatever they like with a cast member's likeness, voice, or even life story. In what ways might producers take advantage of this?

3. Producer Nigel Lythgoe says that it would be foolish for a show's creator to rig a reality show contest and crown a winner against the voters' wishes. Why do you think this might be so?

Chapter 4: Is Reality Television Harmful to Society?

1. Do you think watching violence on reality programs makes a person more likely to be violent in real life? Why or why not?

2. How do you think viewers might react to a nonwhite Bachelor or Bachelorette?

3. Do you think crew members of reality shows should be held responsible if someone they are filming hurts themselves or someone else, and the crew does not try to stop it?

Chapter 5: The Influence and Future of Reality Television

1. The author mentions several scripted television shows and films that have been influenced by reality television. Can you think of others?

2. Why do you think people enjoy interacting on social media outlets such as Twitter and Facebook about the shows they watch?

3. How do you predict reality television will look ten years from now? Which of the many subgroups do you think will be the most popular with future viewers?

ORGANIZATIONS TO CONTACT

American Center for Children and Media (ACCM)
5400 N. St. Louis Ave.
Chicago, IL 60625
Phone: (773) 509-5510
Fax: (773) 509-5303
E-mail: info@centerforchildrenandmedia.org
Website: www.centerforchildrenandmedia.org

The ACCM analyzes research and writings on media and seeks to offer insight and guidance on issues that influence children's media.

American Psychological Association
750 First St. NE
Washington, DC 20002
Phone: (800) 374-2721
Website: www.apa.org

The association studies many aspects of the effects of television (including reality television) on the behavior of people.

Common Sense Media
650 Townsend, Ste. 435
San Francisco, CA 94103
Phone: (415) 863-0600
Fax: (415) 863-0601
Website: www.commonsensemedia.org

This organization makes age-appropriate recommendations for what children should watch. It also seeks to help kids become smart, responsible interpreters of media such as television shows.

New York Reality TV School
520 Hudson St., Ste. PRS
New York, NY 10014
Phone: (646) 372-8666
E-mail: indealcreativeny@gmail.com
Website: www.newyorkrealitytvschool.com

The New York Reality TV School offers classes and seminars in how best to prepare to audition for a reality program.

Parents Television Council
707 Wilshire Blvd., Ste. 2075
Los Angeles, CA 90017
Phone: (800) 882-6868
Fax: (213) 403-1301
Website: www.parentstv.org

This organization monitors prime-time television programs and helps parents decide whether a show is appropriate for children to watch or not.

Books

Troy DeVolld. *Reality TV: An Insider's Guide to TV's Hottest Market*. Studio City, CA: Michael Wiese, 2011. The author gives an overview of the history and types of reality programs and then discusses in depth how to produce a reality show.

Michael Essany. *Reality Check: The Business and Art of Producing Reality TV*. Burlington, MA: Focal, 2008. Recommended for older children, this book explains the business and process of producing a reality television program.

Internet Sources

Keith Hollihan. "The Omarosa Experiment." *Morning News*, January 17, 2006. www.themorningnews.org/article/the-omarosa-experiment. Hollihan's article focuses on the mental screening cast members go through to get cast on reality shows. It features interviews with well-known reality personalities and the psychologists who evaluated them.

James Poniewozik. "Why Reality TV Is Good for Us." *Time*, February 12, 2003. www.time.com/time/magazine/article/0,9171,421047,00.html. This article examines some of the positive aspects and effects of reality television.

Steven Reiss and James Wiltz. "Why America Loves Reality TV." *Psychology Today*, September 1, 2001. www.psychologytoday.com/articles/200109/why-america-loves-reality-tv. This article summarizes and simplifies Steven Reiss's findings on the motivations of people who watch reality television.

Kendon Willis. "Ten Things Reality TV Won't Tell You." *SmartMoney*, April 10, 2009. www.smartmoney.com/spend/rip-offs/10-things-reality-tv-wont-tell-you-22427. This article focuses on how producers manipulate reality shows and on the dangers that cast (and crew) members sometimes face.

Websites

Reality Blurred (www.realityblurred.com). This website features articles on reality television programs and reviews and analyzes them.

Reality Check by Gina (http://realitycheckbygina.blogspot .com). Although this site has not been updated since 2007, it contains many interviews with reality show participants that were conducted by a former radio DJ.

Reality TV World (www.realitytvworld.com). This site features current news articles about a variety of reality shows.

Videojug.com (www.videojug.com/tag/tv). This site offers several video interviews with a reality show producer. He explains many aspects of the reality business, from coming up with an idea for a show to the actual production of one.

INDEX

PICTURE CREDITS

Cover: © Monkey Business Images/Shutterstock.com

© A&E/The Kobal Collection, 75

© Alexander Joe/AFP/Getty Images, 26

© AP Images /Ann Johansson, 29

© AP Images/Gus Ruelas, 80

© AP Images/Peter Kramer, 64

© Araya Diaz/Getty Images for TechCrunch, 89

© Bill Inoshita/CBS Photo Archive via Getty Images, 19

© Bravo TV/The Kobal Collection/ Zink, Vivian, 67

© CBS Photo Archive/Getty Images, 15

© China Photos/Getty Images, 24

© Chip Somodevilla/Getty Images, 93

© Christopher Polk/Getty Images for NBCUniversal, 49

© Denise Truscello, 72

© Ethan Miller/Getty Images, 74

© FilmMagic/Getty Images, 52

© Fox via Getty Images, 8, 33, 61

© Frederick M. Brown/Getty Images, 12

© Gale, Cengage Learning, 23, 41

© Golden Pixels LLC/Alamy, 43

© HBO/The Kobal Collection, 63

© Ian Dagnall/Alamy, 87

© Kristian Dowling/Getty Images, 46

ABOUT THE AUTHOR

Shannon Kelly lives in New York City and is employed in the entertainment business. In addition to her full-time job, she has also worked as a copy editor and development editor on a multitude of reference books over the last decade. In her spare time she enjoys photography, traveling, and watching lots and lots of television.